MY CRAFT BOOK

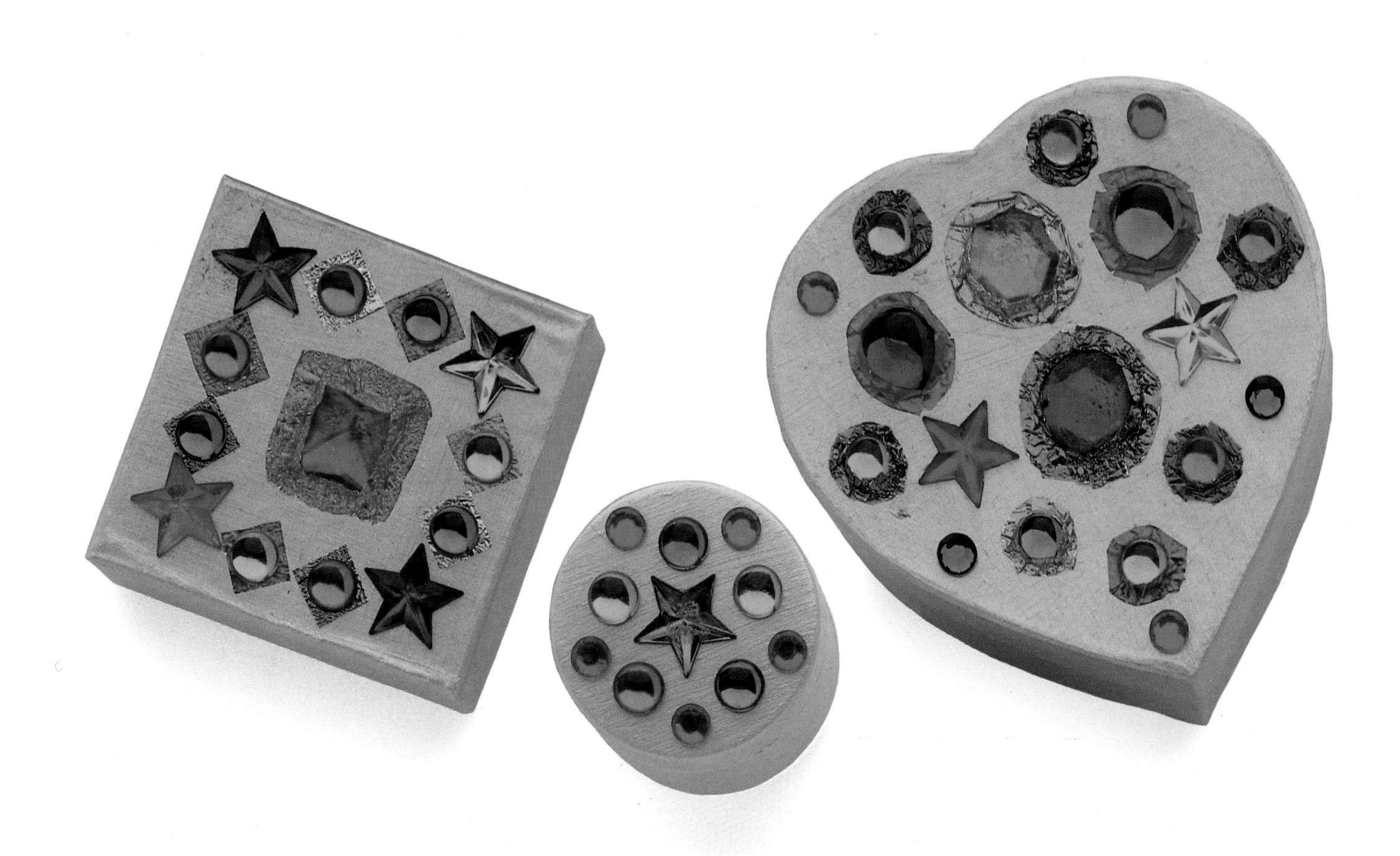

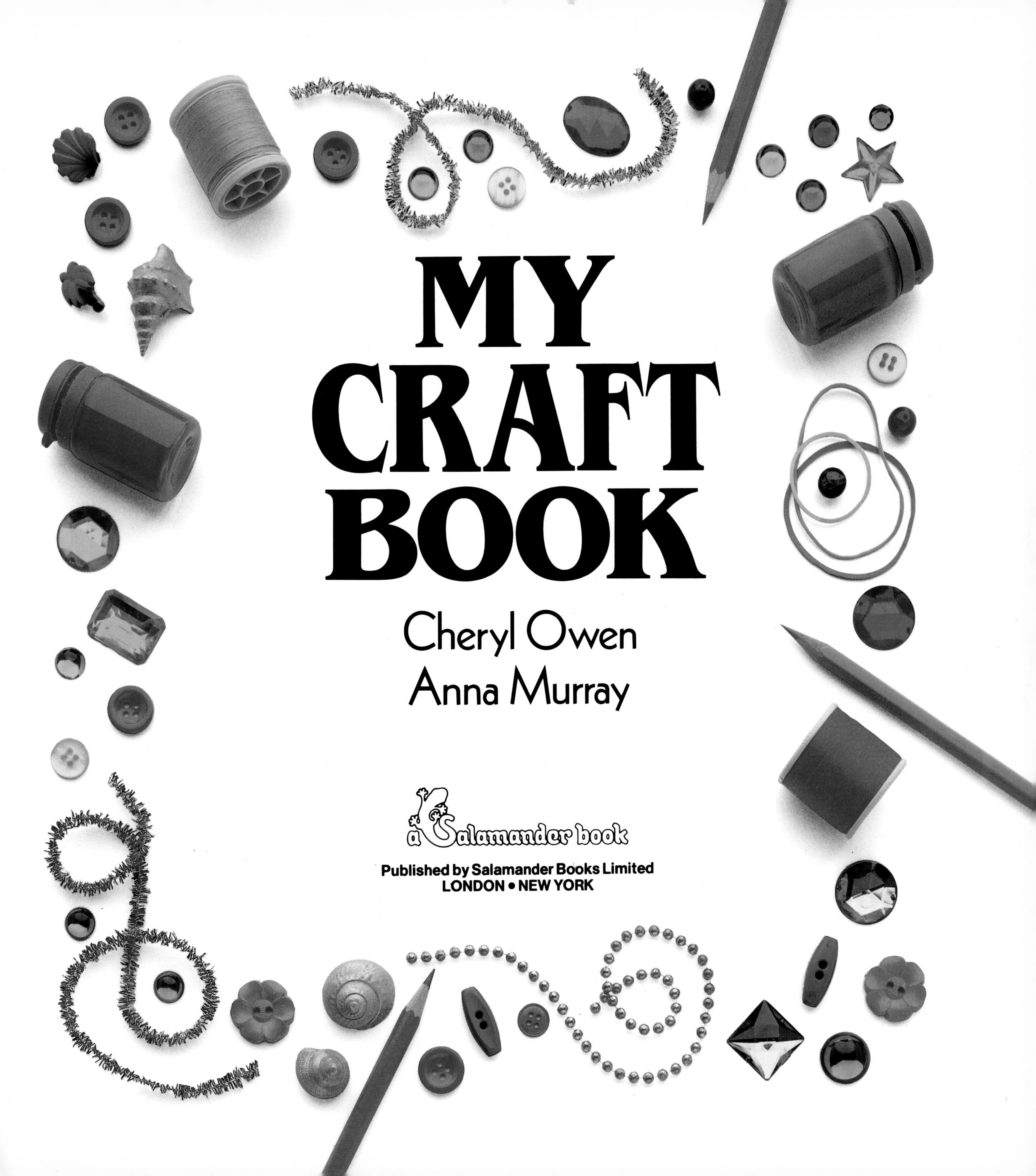

MY CRAFT BOOK

Cheryl Owen
Anna Murray

a Salamander book

Published by Salamander Books Limited
LONDON • NEW YORK

A SALAMANDER BOOK

Published by Salamander Books Ltd.,
129-137 York Way,
London N7 9LG,
England.

ISBN 1 85600 014 1

Distributed by Hodder and Stoughton Services,
PO Box 6, Mill Road, Dunton Green,
Sevenoaks, Kent TN13 2XX.

CREDITS

Managing editor: Veronica Ross
Art director: Rachael Stone
Photographer: Jonathan Pollock
Assistant photographer: Peter Cassidy
Editor: Coral Walker
Designer: Alison Watson
Illustrator: John Hutchinson
Character illustrator: Jo Gapper
Diagram artist: Malcolm Porter
Typeset by: Ian Palmer
Colour separation by: P & W Graphics, Pte., Singapore
Printed in Italy

CONTENTS

INTRODUCTION

Welcome to *My Craft Book* – pages and pages of fabulous projects for you to make, each one with easy-to-follow instructions and colourful step-by-step pictures to help you. Learn how to tie-dye, make greetings cards, glove puppets, papier mâché bowls and paper jewellery. And don't just make the projects for yourself – nearly everything in this book will make an ideal present for a friend or someone in your family.

BEFORE YOU BEGIN

- Do check with an adult before starting any projects; you might need their help.
- Read the instructions before you begin.
- Gather together all the items you need first.
- Cover the work surface with newspaper or an old cloth.
- Protect your clothes with an apron or wear very old clothes.

WHEN YOU HAVE FINISHED

- Tidy everything away. Store special pens, paints, glue etc in old ice-cream containers or biscuit tins.
- Wash paintbrushes and remember to put the tops back on pens, paints and glue containers.

SAFETY FIRST!

Do use your common sense when using anything hot or sharp. You will be able to make most of the projects yourself, but sometimes you will need help. Look out for the SAFETY TIP. It appears on those projects where you will need to ask an adult for help.

But, please remember the basic rules of safety:

- Never leave scissors open or lying around where smaller children can reach them.
- Always stick needles and pins into a pin cushion or a scrap of cloth when you are not using them.
- Never use an oven, iron or craft knife without the help or supervision of an adult.

EQUIPMENT

Every project will list all the things you need; for many of them, you will simply need to hunt around the house, but do check with an adult before taking anything. Some items, such as jewellery fittings and fabric paints, will need to be bought from a craft supplier or large department store.

USING PATTERNS

At the back of the book you will find the patterns you will need to make many of the projects in the book. Using a pencil, trace the pattern you need. If you are making a project with fabric, cut the pattern out and pin it on to the fabric. Cut out the shape. If you want to cut the pattern out of card, turn your tracing over and rub firmly over the pattern outline with a pencil. The pattern will transfer on to the card. Cut out this shape.

Once you have gained confidence making some of the projects in this book, go on to adapt the ideas to create your own designs. If you enjoy drawing, try making up your own patterns and designs freehand.

GROWN-UPS TAKE NOTE

Every project in *My Craft Book* has been designed with simplicity, yet effectiveness, in mind. However, some potentially dangerous items such as sharp knives and irons do need to be used occasionally. Your involvement will depend on the ability of the child, but we do recommend that you read through any project before it is undertaken.

HUNGRY LIONS

These amusing lion greetings cards have a gift attached – a bright balloon that can easily be removed to play with. Remember that a craft knife is *very* sharp; do ask an adult to help you use it.

1 Cut out a rectangle of orange card 35cm x 18cm (14in x 7in). Score down the centre of the card with scissor points or a craft knife. Fold the card in half.

YOU WILL NEED

Orange and yellow card
Red or pink balloon
Craft knife and scissors
Black felt-tip pen
All-purpose glue
Tracing paper
Ruler and pencil

2 Using a pencil, trace the lion pattern on page 87. Turn the tracing over and hold it in position on the orange card. Rub firmly over the outline of the lion's mane with a pencil. The pattern will appear on the card. Cut around the mane, but do not cut along the fold.

3 Follow the instructions in step 2 to trace the lion's face. Cut the face from yellow card. Draw on the features with a felt-tip pen. Glue the face in position to the front of the card.

4 Open the card out flat and, with scissors or a craft knife, carefully cut along the mouth. Push the balloon out of the mouth so it sticks out like a tongue.

PAPER FLOWERS

These colourful paper flowers make lovely presents. Tie them into a bunch with a huge crêpe paper bow to make a pretty posy. Make a second bunch to keep for yourself to brighten up your room all the year round.

YOU WILL NEED

Brightly coloured crêpe paper
Pipe cleaners
Garden sticks
All-purpose glue
Scissors
Tracing paper and pencil
Pins

1 To make the centre of the flower cut a strip of crêpe paper 30 x 4cm (12 x 1½in). Cut a fringe along one end and spread a line of glue along the opposite edge.

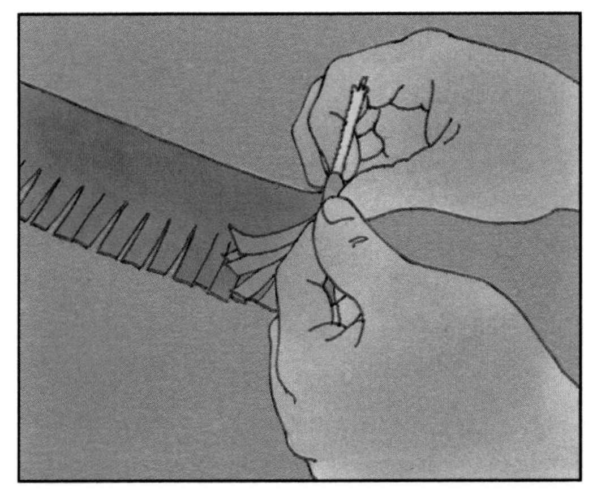

2 Cut a pipe cleaner in half and carefully wrap the glued edge of the crêpe paper around the top of the pipe cleaner. Fan out the paper fringe.

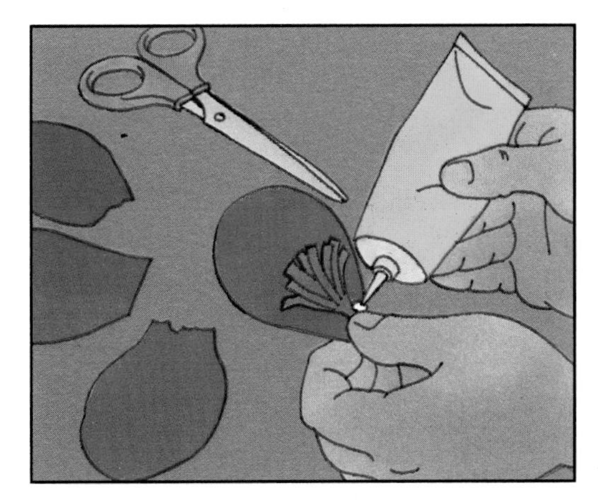

3 Trace the petal pattern on page 87 and cut it out. Pin the pattern to five layers of different coloured crêpe paper and cut around it. Dab glue on the base of each petal and stick the petals one at a time around the bottom end of the flower centre.

4 To attach the stem, hold the pipe cleaner firmly against a garden stick and wrap the two together with a 1cm (½in) wide strip of crêpe paper. Glue the ends to secure them in place.

BUTTON GIFT TAGS

Pretty buttons are used to make these unusual gift tags. Add one to a birthday present for a special friend, and at Christmas try using sparkly buttons with glittery cards.

1 Cut out a rectangle of card for each gift tag. The card can be folded in half, or even cut to a different shape, if you prefer.

2 Glue on other pieces of coloured card to look like a landscape or beach, and add details with a felt-tip pen. Alternatively, leave the gift tag plain.

3 Arrange buttons on the gift tag in an attractive pattern then either glue or sew them securely in place.

4 Punch a hole at the top of the gift tag and thread with narrow ribbon. A ribbon bow can also be glued on.

LIZZIE THE LIZARD

You will be the centre of attention when you take this fabulous pet lizard out for a walk. Attach a wire lead to its neck and it will wriggle and squirm just like a real lizard when you pull it along.

YOU WILL NEED

Large piece of foam rubber
Large scissors
Pins
Poster paints and large brush
Tracing paper and pencil
Felt-tip pen
Thick wire

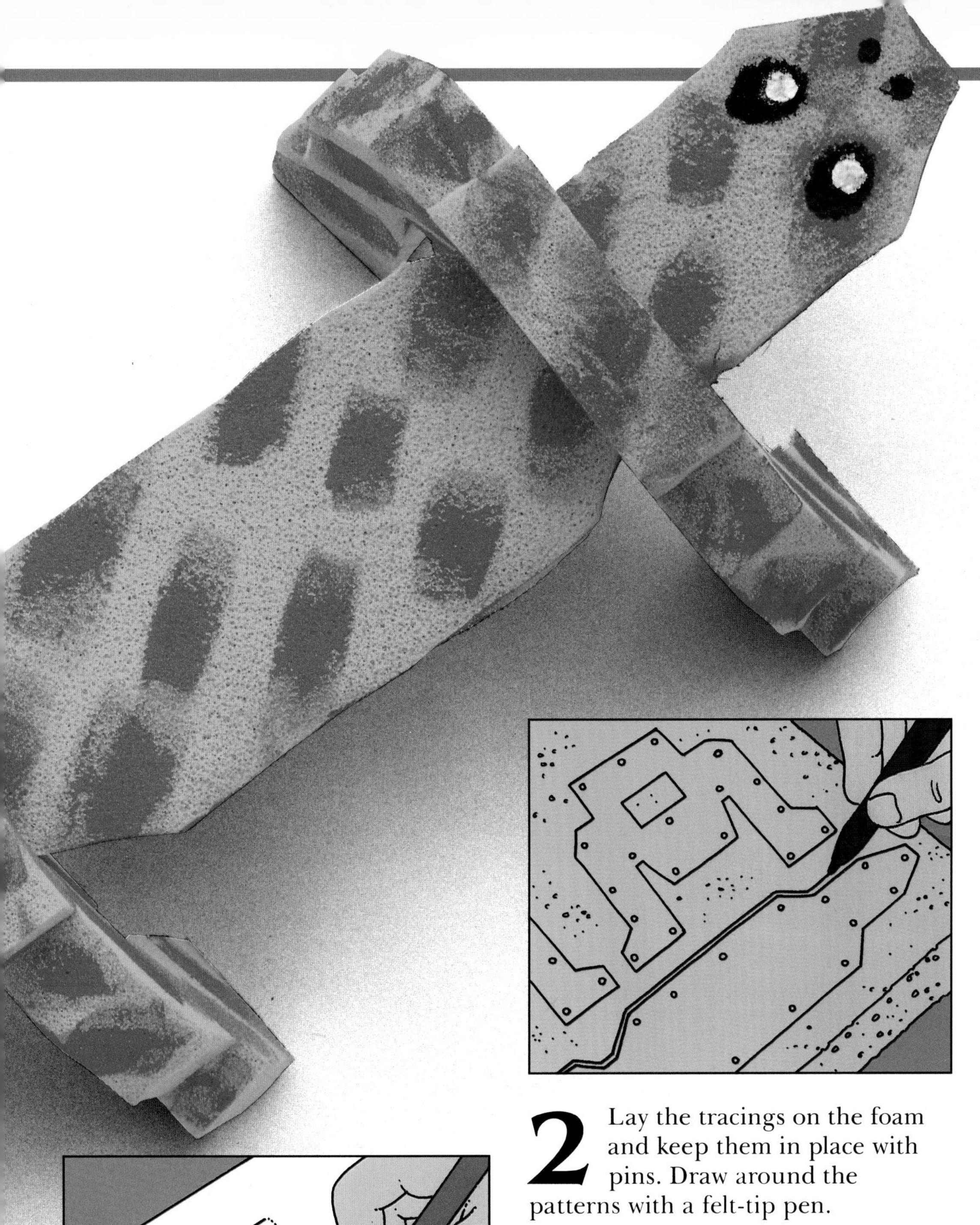

SAFETY TIP: *Make sure an adult helps you to make a lead for your lizard.*

1 Trace the lizard body once and the lizard legs twice, from the patterns on pages 86 and 87 and cut them out. Cut out the area in the centre of the legs.

2 Lay the tracings on the foam and keep them in place with pins. Draw around the patterns with a felt-tip pen.

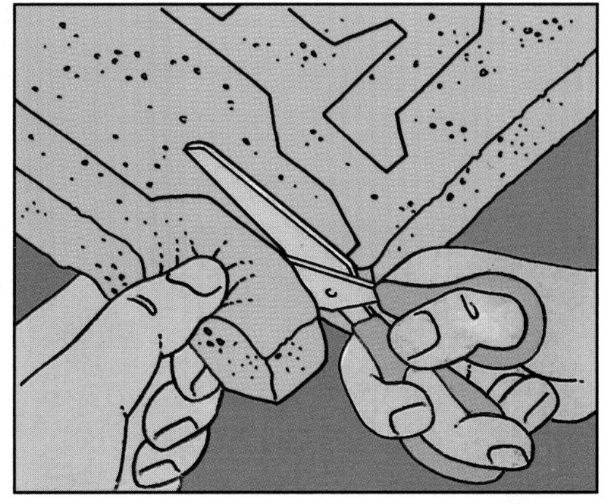

3 Cut the foam shapes out with scissors, cut the hole in the legs. Paint the shapes in bright colours and leave them to dry.

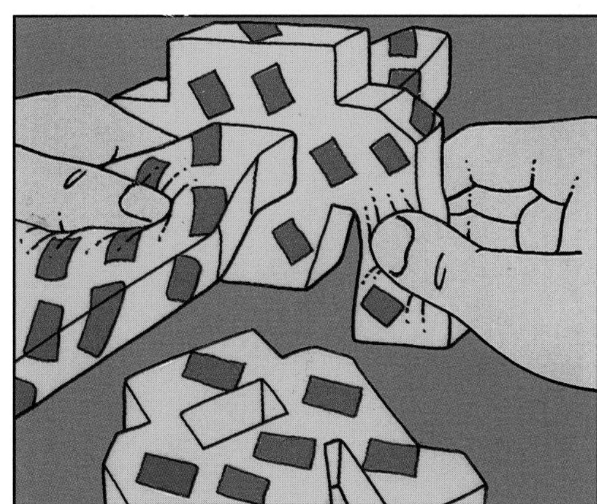

4 Slip the legs on to the body. Ask an adult to help you make a lead for your lizard. Make a loop at one end of a length of wire. Slip the lizard's head into the wire loop. Move it along and watch it wiggle and walk on its lead.

NOVELTY PEN ENDS

YOU WILL NEED
Modelling clay that will harden in the oven
Modelling clay varnish
Pencils and pipe cleaners
Rolling pin and blunt knife
Knitting needle
All-purpose glue

Be the envy of all your classmates with these novelty pen ends made from coloured modelling clay. Once you have made the shapes here, you can think of others to try. Make sure your hands are clean when making the pen ends as any dirt will come off on to the clay.

SAFETY TIP: *Make sure an adult helps you when using the oven.*

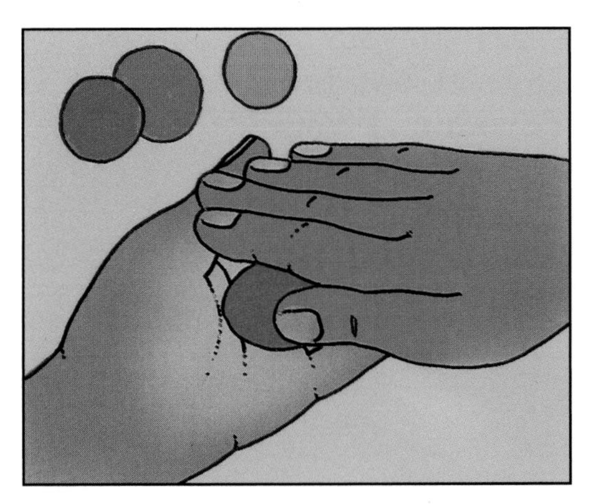

1 All of the shapes are made by rolling the clay into a ball or tube. Start with a piece of clay about the size of a large marble and roll it in the palm of your hand until it is soft enough to shape.

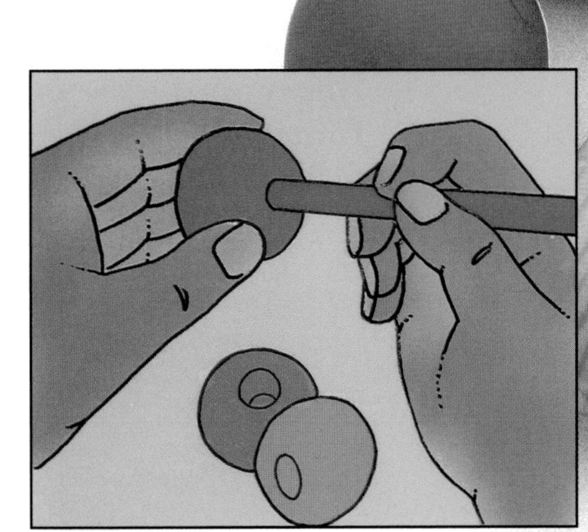

2 For the spider, mouse, bird and fish, roll the clay into a ball, push the end of a pencil into the clay ball to make the hole that it will sit on. Lightly pat the clay back into shape.

3 With the knitting needle, press small holes into the clay ball for the legs, tails or feathers. Roll out another small piece of clay and shape details like eyes or ears and gently press them into place. For the spider, add a second ball for the head.

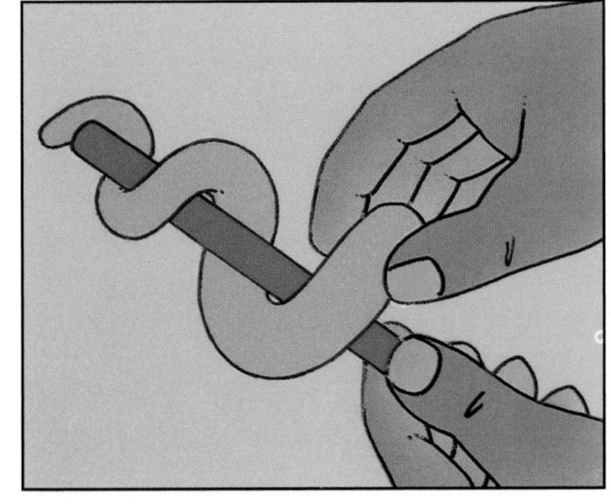

4 To make the snake, hot dog or carrot, roll the clay into tubes. For the hot dog, slice a brown tube down its length as you would a bread roll, add a smaller red tube for the sausage. Squash the carrot into a point at one end and add leaves. Twist a green tube around a pencil to shape it into a snake.

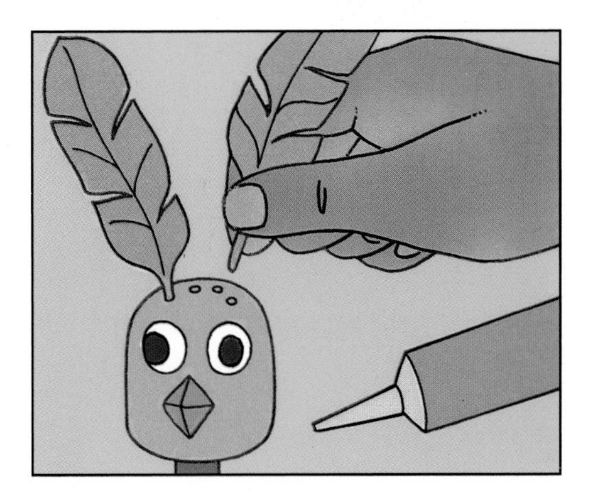

5 Ask an adult to help you bake the pen ends in an oven, following the instructions on the packet. When baked and cool, varnish the clay. Once dry, glue the feathers or pipe cleaners in the holes to make the legs, tails and other features.

GLOVE PUPPETS

A glove puppet is made to fit on your hand – a bit like a real glove except that it looks like a character or an animal. Your fingers make the puppet move and do funny things. This glove puppet is made to look like a clown, with a big, smiling grin.

1 To make the head, scrunch up some newspaper into a ball. Cut off a length of cardboard tube 5cm (2in) long. Use masking tape to stick the paper ball on top of the tube, then cover the ball and tube with more strips of masking tape. Paint the head and tube white. Leave to dry and then paint on the face.

YOU WILL NEED
Newspaper and cardboard tube
2.5cm (1in) wide masking tape
Wool and felt scraps
20cm (1/8 yd) cotton fabric
Poster paints and paintbrushes
Scissors and fabric glue
Needle and thread
Chalk and ribbon

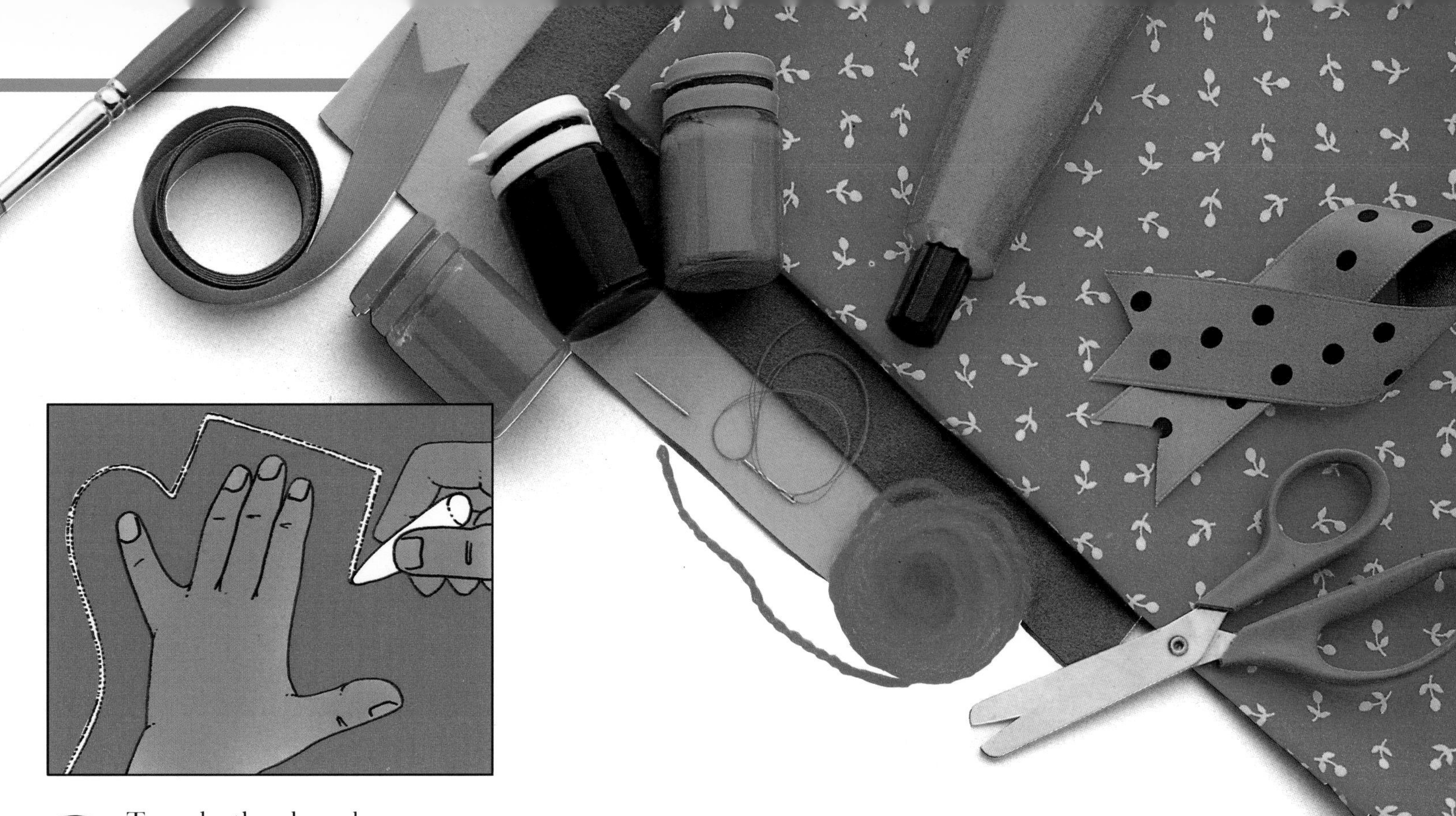

2 To make the glove, lay your hand on the fabric, as shown in the diagram. Using the chalk, draw a line around your hand about 5cm (2in) away. Draw a straight line across the top edge and the lower edge. Cut out two of these shapes from fabric.

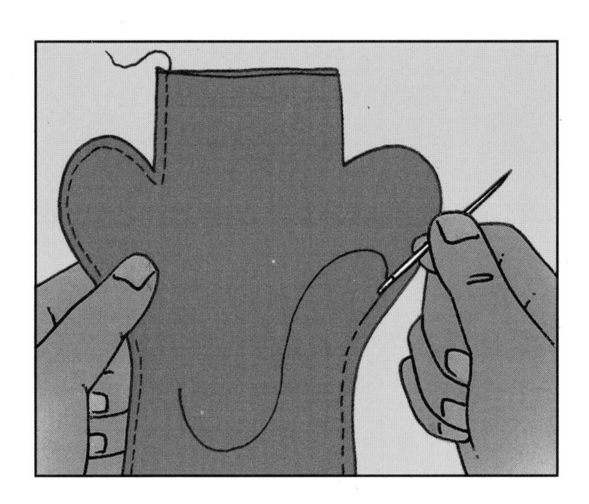

3 Place the fabric, right sides together, and sew up the sides of the shape. Do not sew across the lower edge or the neck opening. Turn the fabric to the right side and hem the lower edge.

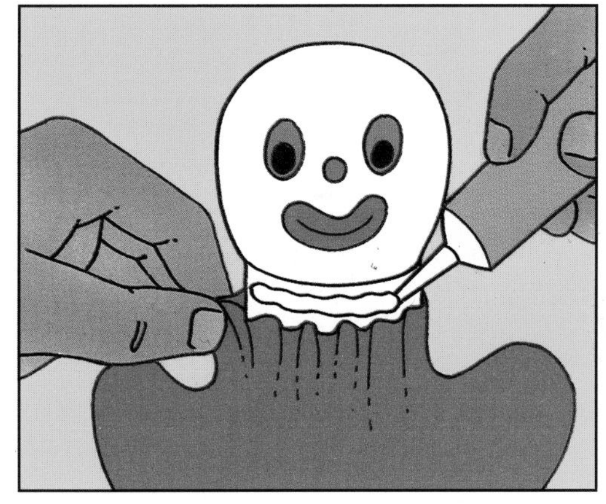

4 Push the neck opening on to the tube and glue it in place. Decorate the front of the clown with felt buttons and tie a ribbon around the clown's neck, to hide the join.

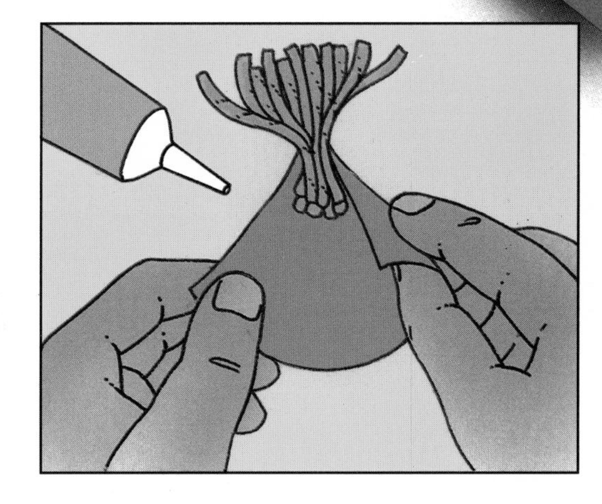

5 For the hair, loop some wool around your fingers, then tie it at the centre with extra wool. Make several wool loops and glue them around the clown's head. To make the hat, trace the pattern on page 88 and cut out. Pin the tracing on to felt and cut out. Glue a few loops of wool to the top corner. Overlap the straight edges, trapping the looped ends of wool inside. Glue the edges together, and glue the hat to the clown's head.

SHELL JEWELLERY

Next time you go on holiday to the beach, collect some shells to decorate hair combs, slides and brooches for pretty hair and fashion accessories. Once your friends see them, you'll probably be asked to make more!

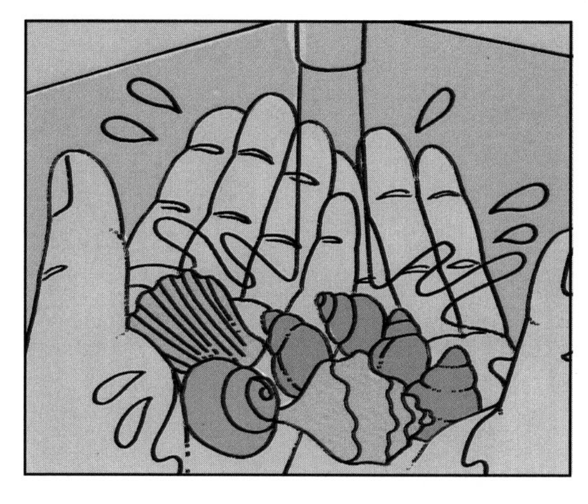

1 Wash the shells to remove any sand or seaweed. Dry them well and lay them out on the sheets of newspaper.

2 Decide what you are going to decorate and plan which shells you will use. Try arranging the shells near the slide or clip to make a pleasing decoration.

4 Ask an adult to help you to glue the shells in place. Dab a little glue to the base of the shell and to the comb or brooch. Let the glue become tacky before sticking them together. Hold the shell in place until the glue has started to set. Repeat to glue all the shells in place.

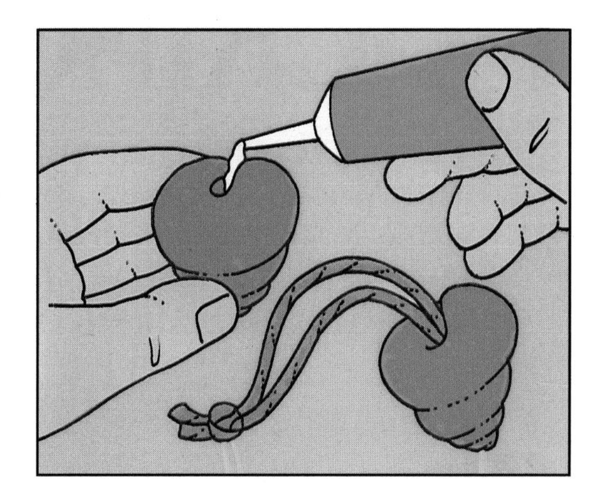

5 To make hair toggles, cut a 15cm (6in) length of elastic and knot the ends together. Choose two similar shells and trickle glue into the hole. Push the knotted end of the elastic into one shell and the opposite end into the other shell. Leave them for the glue to dry.

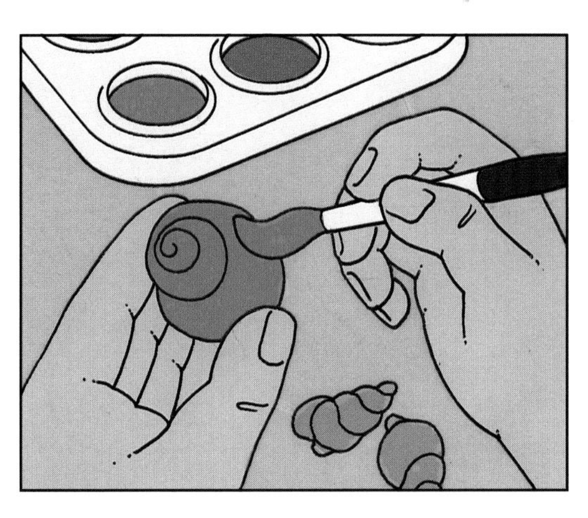

3 Mix the paint with a little water – it is better if the paint is quite thick – then paint the shells. If you want, add a touch of gold paint to some of the shells after the first coat of paint has dried.

ROCKING SHEEP

This sweet pair of sheep will make a great present for a younger brother or sister, or anyone who loves animals. Tap the sheep very lightly and they will gently rock from side to side.

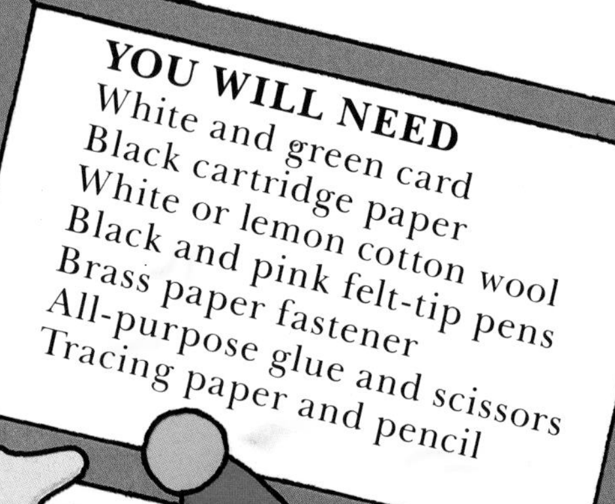

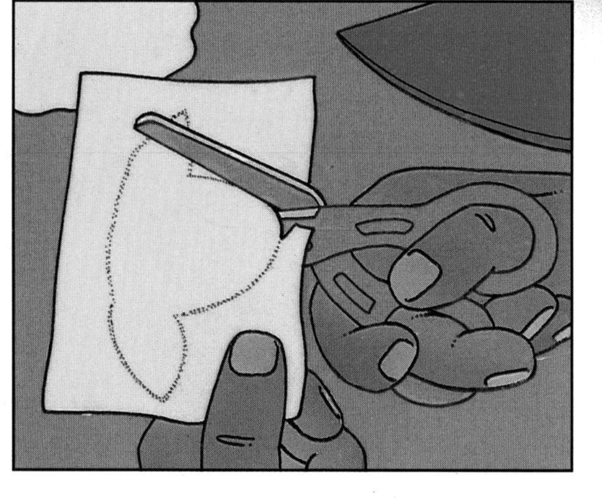

1 Cut out a circle of green card 24cm (9½in) in diameter; fold it in half. Using a pencil, trace the body and head patterns on page 88. Turn the tracing over and position it on the white card. Rub firmly over the outline with a pencil. The body and head patterns will appear on the card. Cut these out.

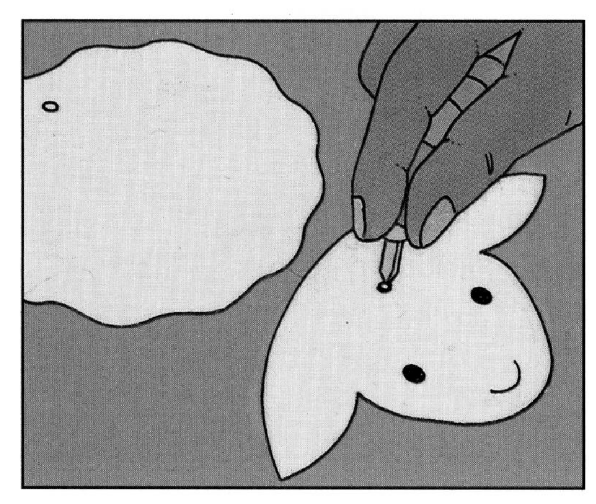

2 Draw the face with felt-tip pens. Make a small hole on the body and head at the dot, as shown. Push a paper fastener through the hole in the head.

3 Glue cotton wool to the body and head between the ears. Loosely fix the head to the body by pushing the paper fastener through the hole in the sheep's body. Open out the prongs at the back.

4 Cut two strips of black paper for the legs. Place the body on the centre of the semi-circle of green card. Glue the legs in position so that the tops of them are hidden by the sheep's body. Glue the sheep on to the green card.

PASTA JEWELLERY

Try turning pasta shapes into colourful, fun jewellery. With a mixture of pasta bows, shells and tubes you can make lots of pretty earrings, bracelets and necklaces. Use felt-tip pens to colour the jewellery to match your outfits.

YOU WILL NEED

Pasta shapes
Earring and brooch fittings
All-purpose glue
Silver string, cord and elastic
Waterproof felt-tip pens
Round elastic

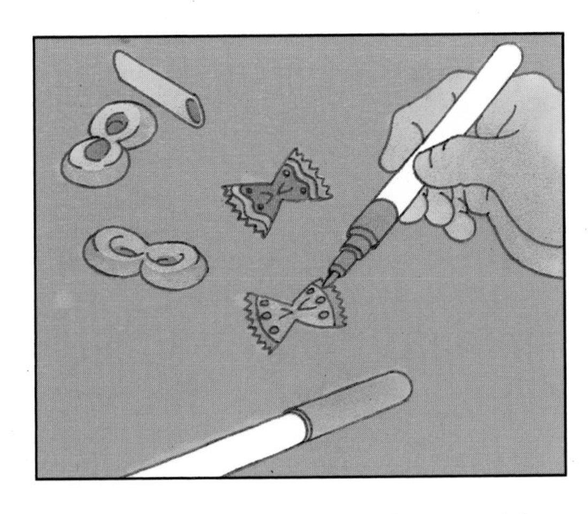

1 Colour the pasta shapes with felt-tip pens. Experiment with spots and stripes and use all sorts of colours to make your own patterns. Leave the pasta to dry.

2 For the necklace and bracelet, cut a long length of silver string. Tie on the pasta shapes leaving 2.5cm (1in) between each piece.

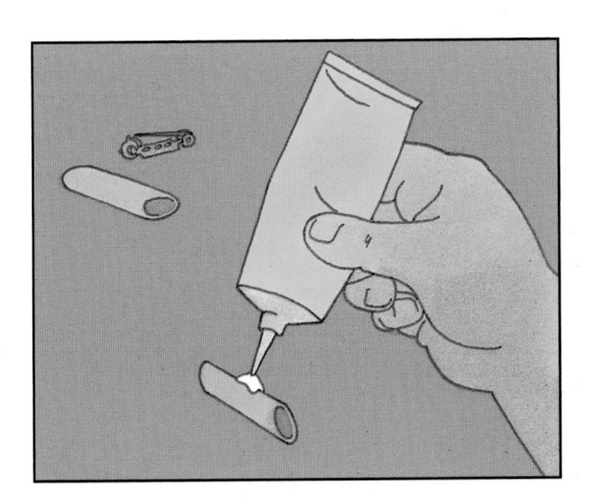

3 To make a brooch, carefully glue together two pasta tubes, and then glue on the brooch back. Put the brooch somewhere safe for the glue to set.

4 For the earrings, tie elastic round the centre of the pasta bow and knot it at the back. Slip the earring wire underneath the elastic to finish.

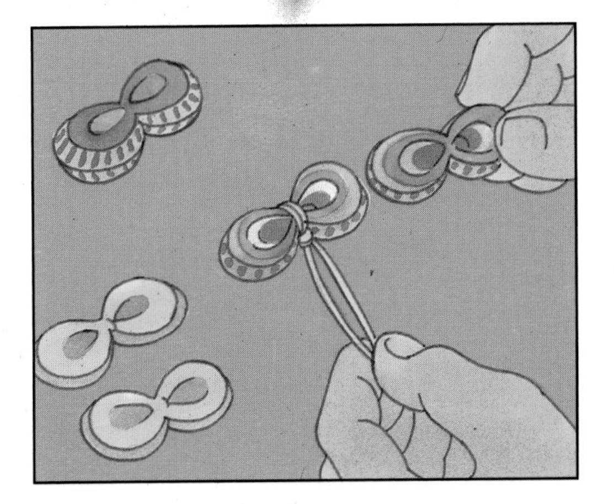

5 Make hair bobbles by glueing four pasta bows back to back in two pairs. Tie each pair of bobbles on to a 10cm (4in) loop of round elastic.

CRAYON EGGS

These colourful eggs would look lovely in a bowl as an Easter decoration or you could thread some on to ribbons to hang at a window. If you are nervous about blowing an egg, you can hard boil it for half an hour instead. Ask an adult to help you do this. Leave the eggs to cool before decorating them.

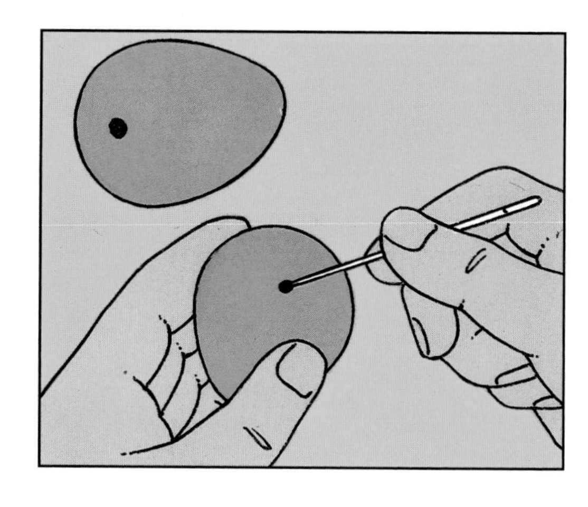

1 Carefully pierce a small hole at each end of an egg with a darning needle. Wiggle the needle to make one hole 6mm (¼in) wide and the other 1cm (⅜in) wide.

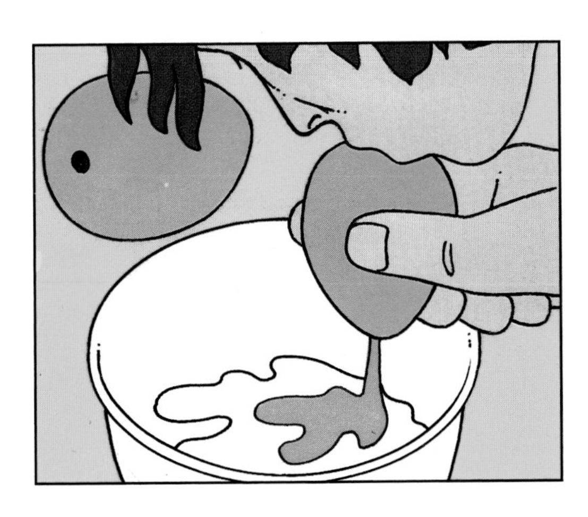

2 Gently push the needle into the egg to break the yoke. Hold the egg over a bowl and blow through the smaller hole until the contents of the egg are emptied into the bowl.

SAFETY TIP: *Make sure an adult helps you prepare the fabric dye.*

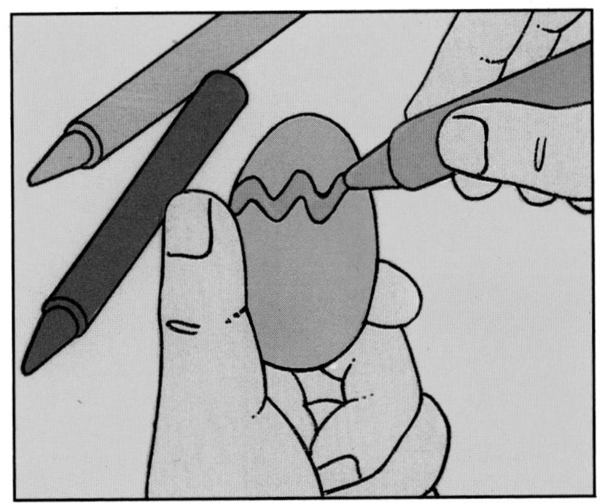

3 Holding the egg very gently, draw patterns on to it with wax crayons. Now ask an adult to help you prepare the fabric dye, following the maker's instructions.

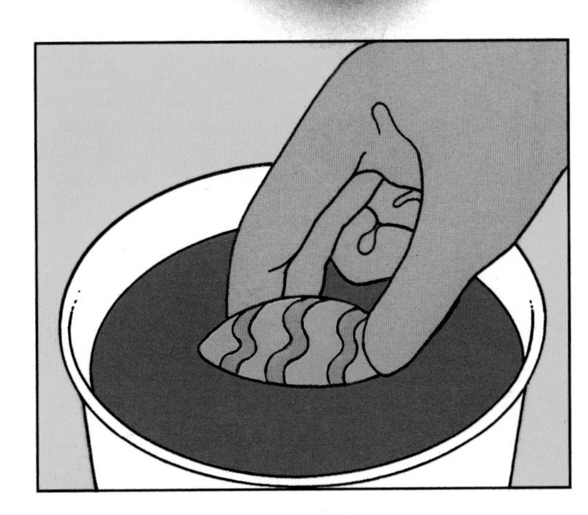

4 Wearing a rubber glove, dip the egg into the dye and hold it under the water until it fills. The dye will stain the egg shell but not the pattern you have made with the wax crayons. Remove the egg after three minutes and rinse.

DANCING BIRDS

Make these jolly bird puppets and treat your friends to a puppet show. By holding the birds from the sticks at the top, you can make them do all sorts of clever antics like tap dancing.

1 Cut one 30cm (12in) and one 20cm (8in) length from the thick wool. Knot the ends of each piece and thread a flat button on to each length.

YOU WILL NEED

Two large round beads
Two small beads
Two flat beads or buttons
Thick and thin wool
Feathers
Blunt needle with large eye
Two sticks
All-purpose glue and scissors

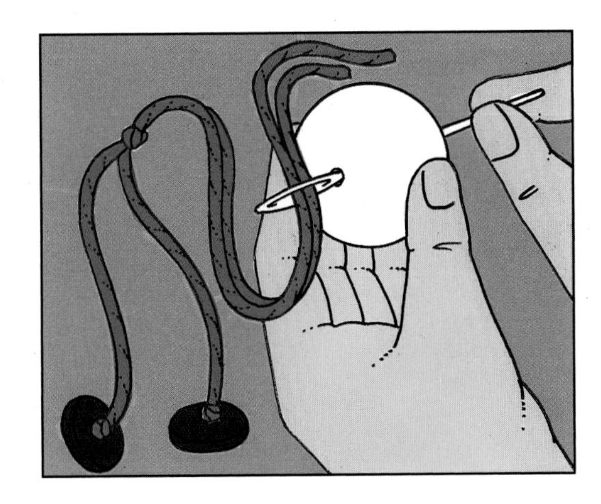

2 Tie another knot close to each button and then knot the two lengths of wool together, 12.5cm (5in) from the buttons. Thread the needle with the two lengths of wool, and then thread on a large round bead. Tie a knot close to it and trim the shorter end of wool.

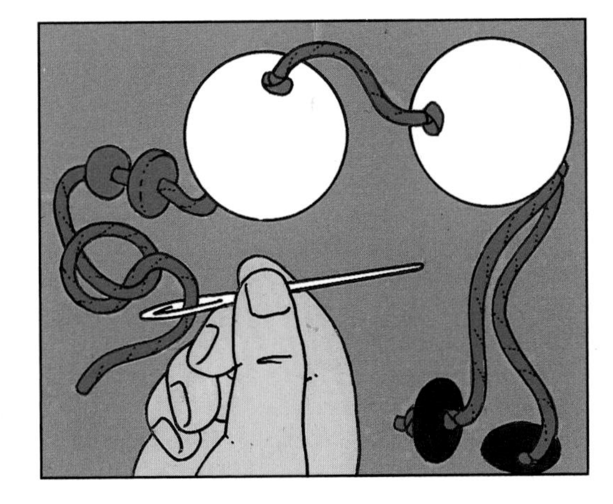

3 Tie a knot 10cm (4in) from the round bead and thread on the second round bead and a small bead. Knot the wool near the small bead and trim the end.

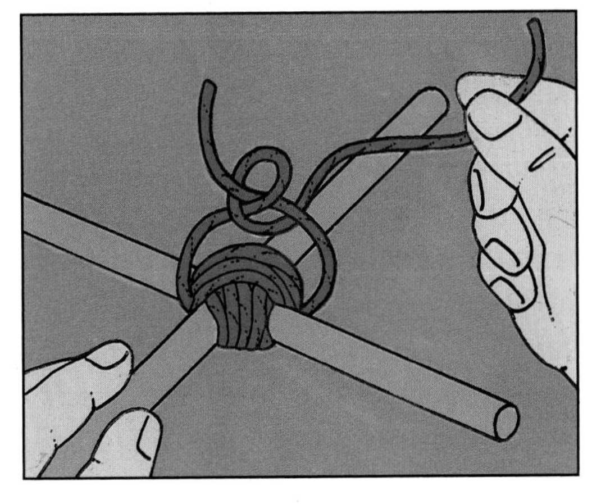

4 Place the sticks in a cross, and tie them together. Use the thin wool to hang the bird from the sticks. Tie a long length of thin wool to each foot. String the feet to the opposite ends of one crossbar. Tie the head to the front stick, and the body to the point where the sticks cross.

5 Glue feathers and felt eyes on to the bird to decorate it. If the beads are plain, paint them in a range of bright colours.

TIE-DYE BAGS

Tie-dye is an exciting way to colour fabric. By tying the fabric in different ways, you can make all kinds of interesting patterns. It is best to use scraps of cotton fabric, as this absorbs the dye more readily. We have made useful little bags, but you can make scarves, hankies or make-up bags.

YOU WILL NEED

Cotton fabric
Fabric dye
Elastic bands and buttons
1cm (3/8in) wide ribbon
Needle, thread and safety pin
Pinking shears

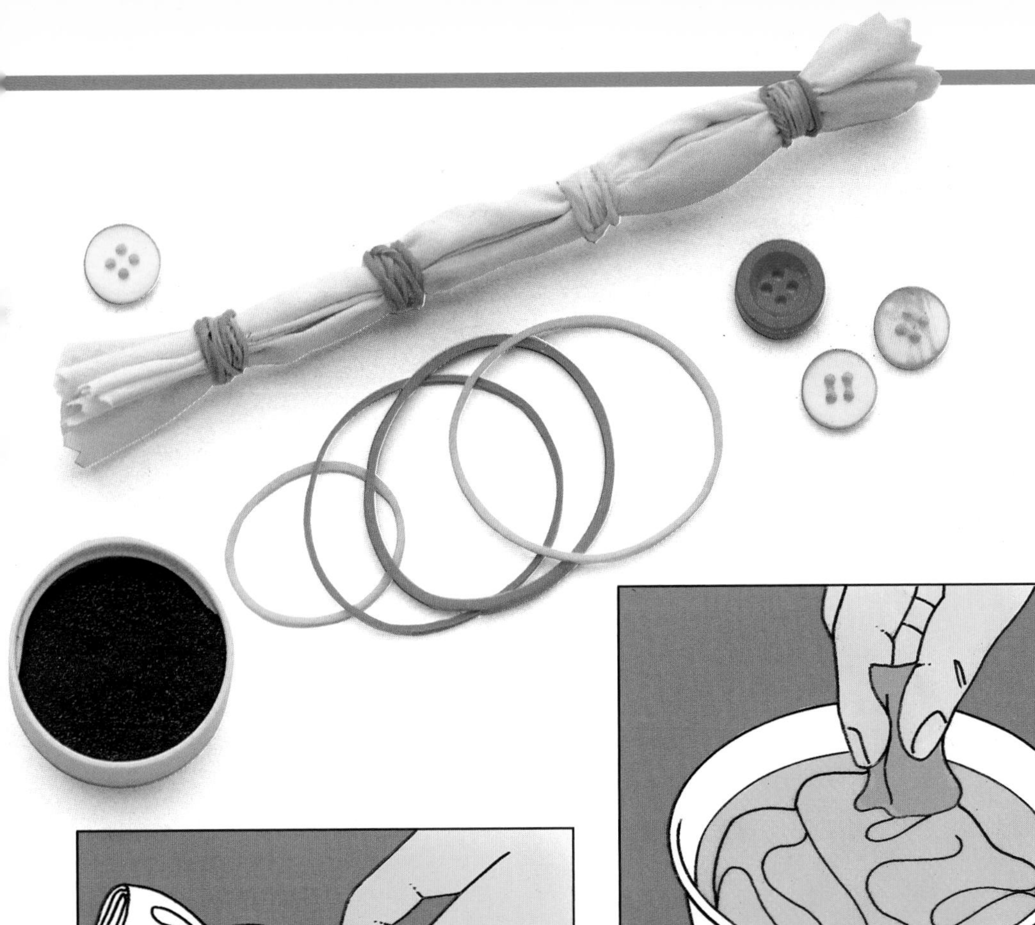

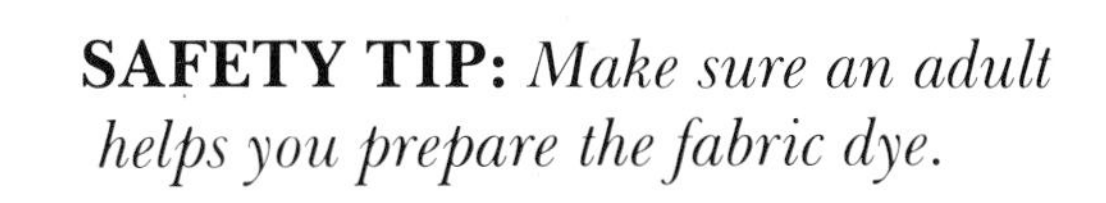

SAFETY TIP: *Make sure an adult helps you prepare the fabric dye.*

1 Fold the fabric into a sausage shape and fasten elastic bands around it at intervals. Or, wrap the fabric around buttons fastening them with elastic bands.

2 Ask an adult to help you dye the fabric following the instructions on the packet. Rinse the fabric and remove the elastic bands. Hang up to dry.

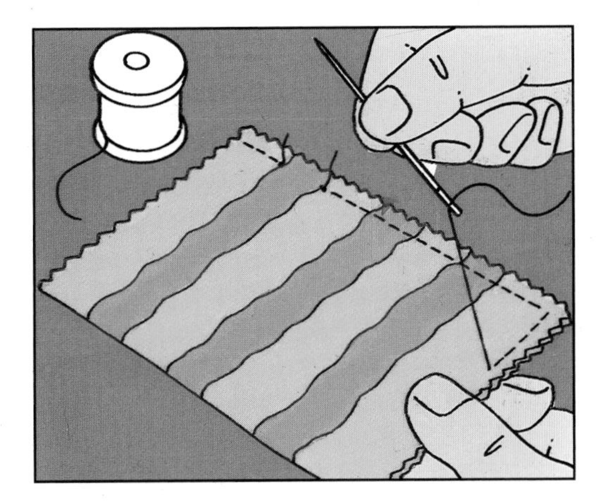

3 To make the little bag, cut a rectangle of fabric about 30.5cm (12in) long by 20cm (8in) wide with pinking shears. Fold the rectangle in half, wrong sides together. Sew a narrow seam up both sides, as shown, leaving a 1.5cm (5/8in) gap, 2.5cm (1in) below the top on the long edge on one side.

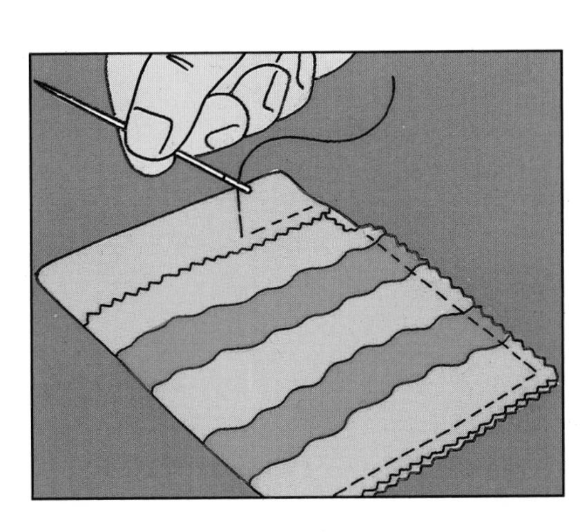

4 Turn down the 2.5cm (1in) of fabric at the top edge of the bag and sew 1cm (3/8in) above the raw edge, as shown, making a channel for the ribbon.

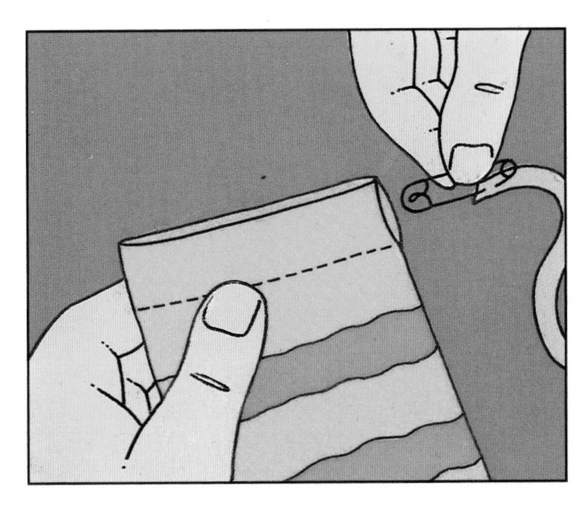

5 Turn the bag the right side out. Thread ribbon through the channel by fixing one end with a safety pin. Knot the ends of the ribbon together and draw it up.

PEBBLE PETS

Gather together some smooth stones of different sizes to make an appealing group of animals and insects. A coat of gloss varnish will protect the painted stones and make them shine.

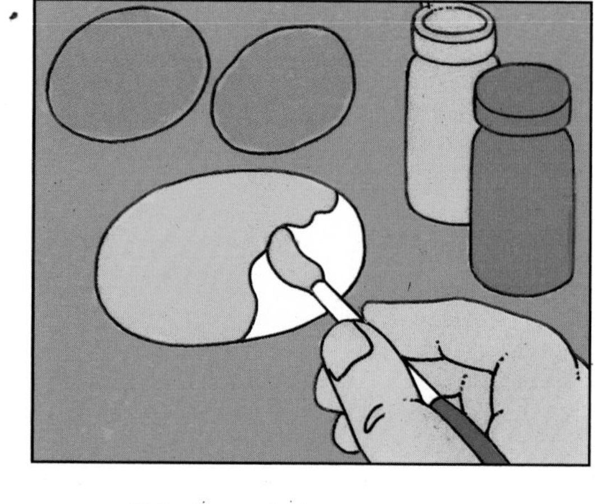

1 Wash and dry the stones thoroughly. Paint them white first and then when they are dry paint on the background colour. Leave to dry in a safe place.

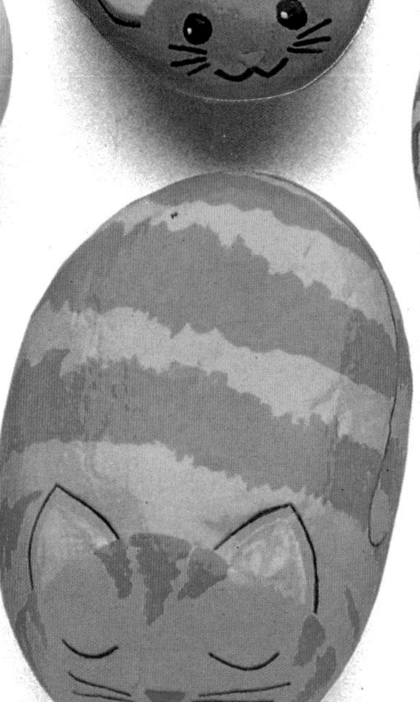

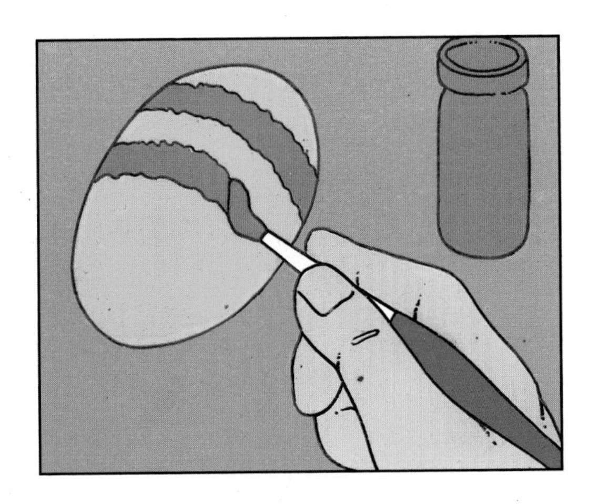

2 Carefully paint the main body markings and details, like the stripes on the cat and spots on the ladybird.

3 Draw the face and small details like whiskers with a felt-tip pen. You could give the stones a coat of varnish at this stage.

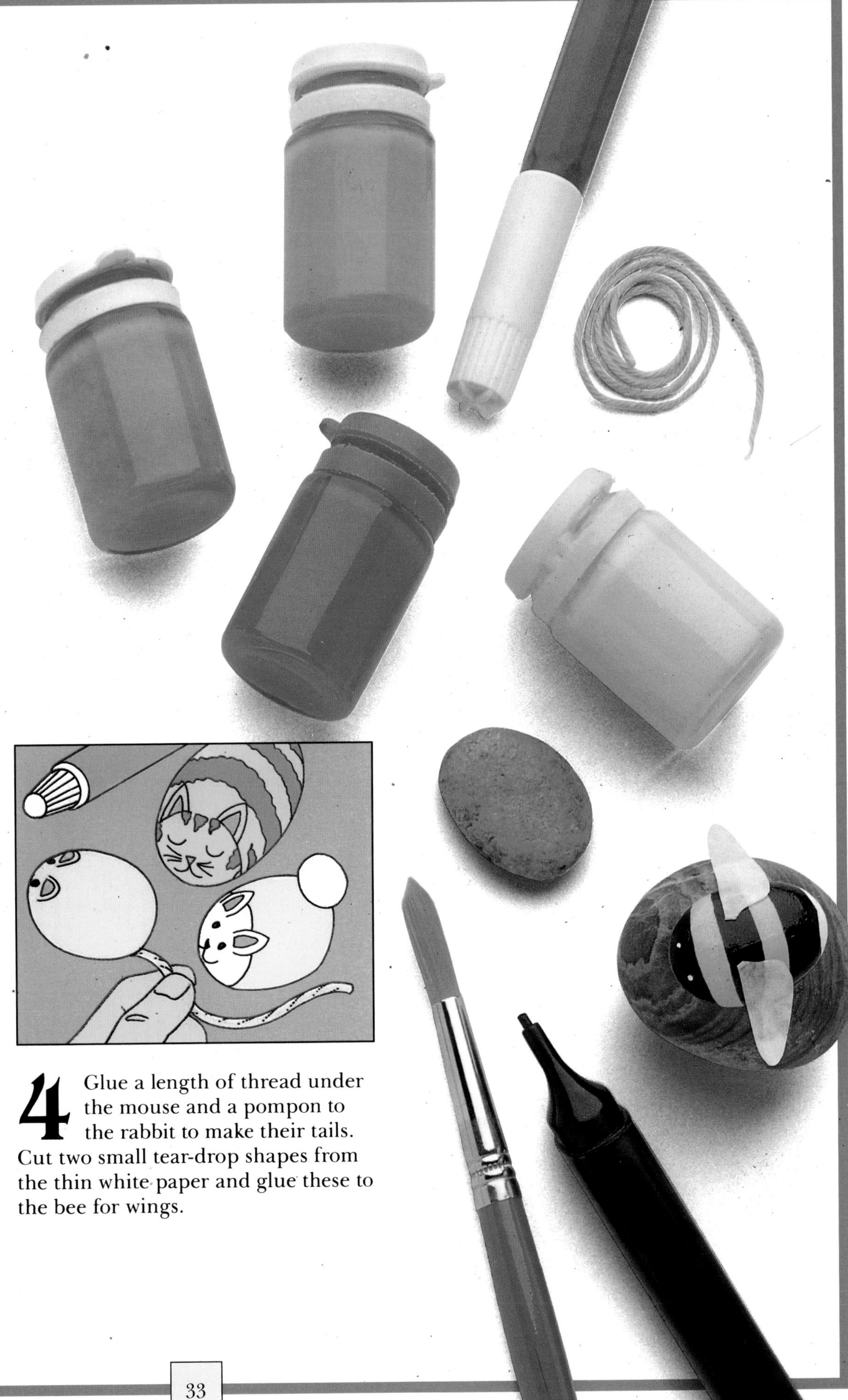

4 Glue a length of thread under the mouse and a pompon to the rabbit to make their tails. Cut two small tear-drop shapes from the thin white paper and glue these to the bee for wings.

PINWHEELS

Watch these colourful pinwheels spin in the breeze. They would look very pretty placed among houseplants on a windowsill, or arranged in a vase.

1 Stick the gummed paper squares together. Cut into the square diagonally from each corner. Make sure you stop cutting when you are 1cm (3/8in) from the centre of the square.

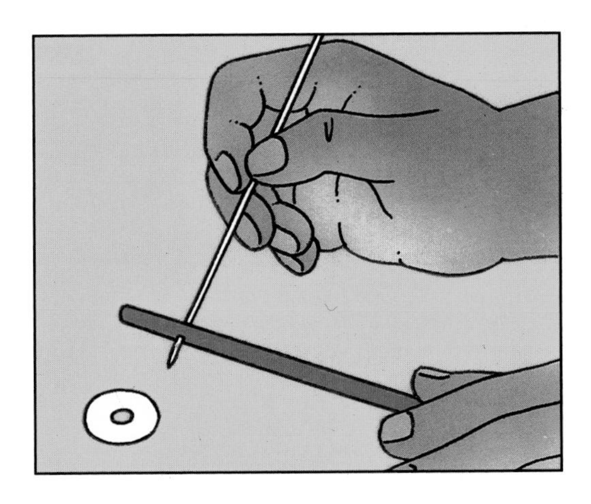

2 Cut out a circle of corrugated card 2.5cm (1in) in diameter; make a hole through the centre. Now make a hole at one end of the straw with some sharp scissor points. Ask an adult to help you do this.

SAFETY TIP:
Make sure an adult helps you when using sharp scissors.

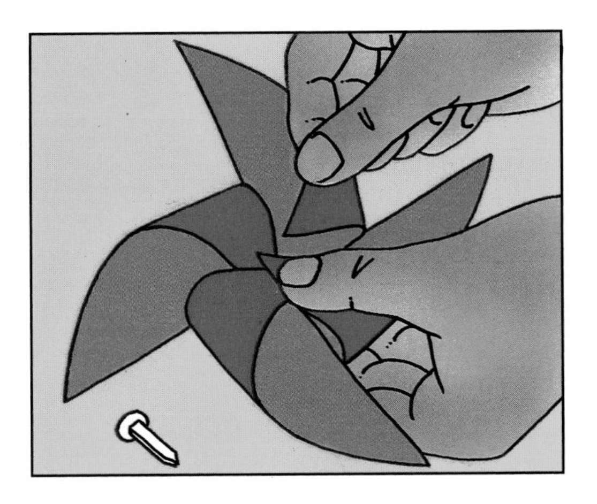

3 Bend every other point of the square over to the centre, as shown, then carefully make a hole through the centre of the pinwheel with scissor points. Ask an adult to help you do this.

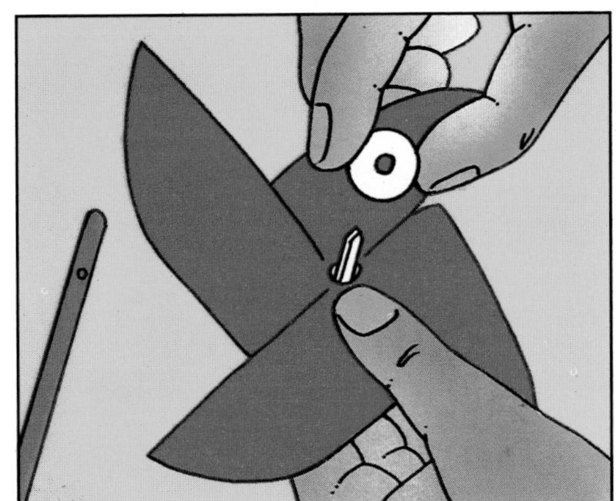

4 Push the paper fastener prongs through the centre of the pinwheel then through the card and straw. Open out the prong ends on the other side of the straw keeping the pinwheel quite loose.

HALLOWEEN MASKS

These spooky masks are a terrific disguise for you to wear at a Halloween party. Decorate them with lots of shiny ribbon and sequins and you'll make quite a scene.

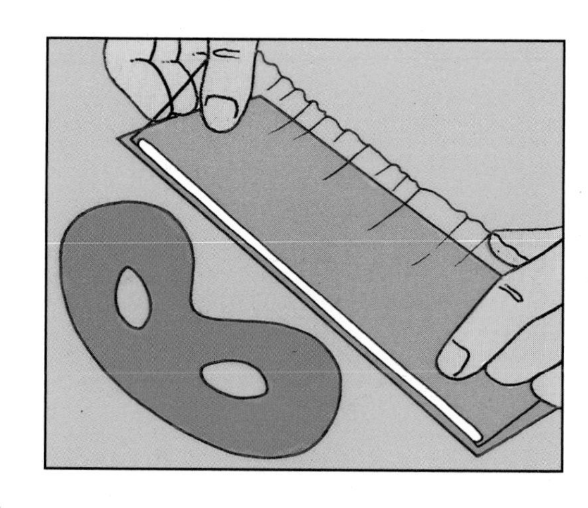

1 Using a pencil, trace the mask pattern on page 89. Turn the tracing over and position it on the card. Rub firmly over the outline with a pencil. The pattern will appear on the card. Cut out the shape. Cut a strip of crêpe paper and iridescent film 50cm x 8cm (20in x 3in). Glue together along one edge.

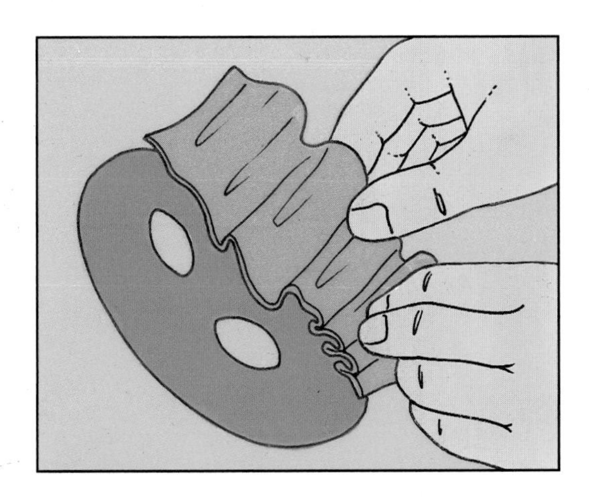

2 Spread glue on the back of the mask above or below the eyes. Take the strip of crêpe paper and iridescent film and press the iridescent film on to the glue, bunching up the strip to fit.

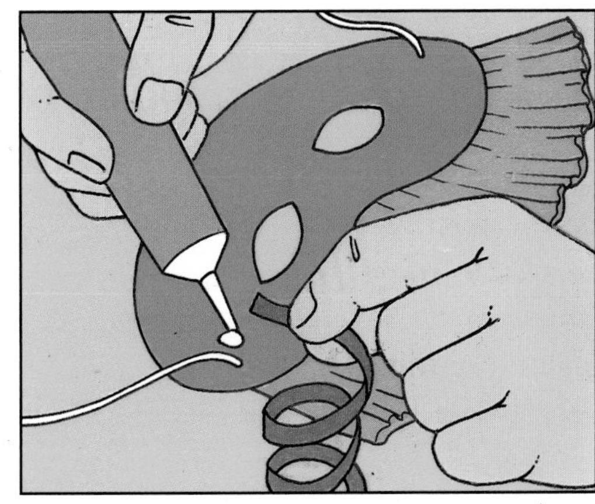

3 Pierce a hole at each side of the mask and thread with elastic; knot the ends. Glue three lengths of curly ribbon to the front of the mask above the holes.

YOU WILL NEED

Coloured card and crêpe paper
Iridescent film
Sequins and curly ribbon
Hat elastic
All-purpose glue
Tracing paper and pencil
Felt-tip pen and scissors

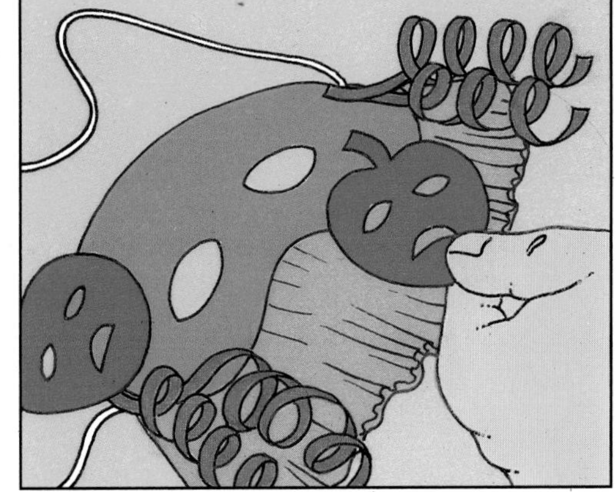

4 Follow the instructions in step 1 to trace the ghost and pumpkin motifs. Cut out either a pair of ghosts or pumpkins. You can cut out their mouths and eyes or simply draw them with a felt-tip pen. Glue the motifs to the mask then glue on lots of sequins to finish.

OCEAN ANIMALS

These ocean animal beanbags are easy to make using simple sewing skills. Add white ribbon to the top of the whale to make it look as though it's spouting water. The starfish is made in the same way as the whale from yellow tie-dyed fabric. **Turn to page 30 to find out how to tie-dye.**

1 To make the whale, trace the patterns on page 88 and cut out. Fold the fabric in half, right sides together. Lay the tracing on the fabric and keep in place with sticky tape or pins. Cut out the shape.

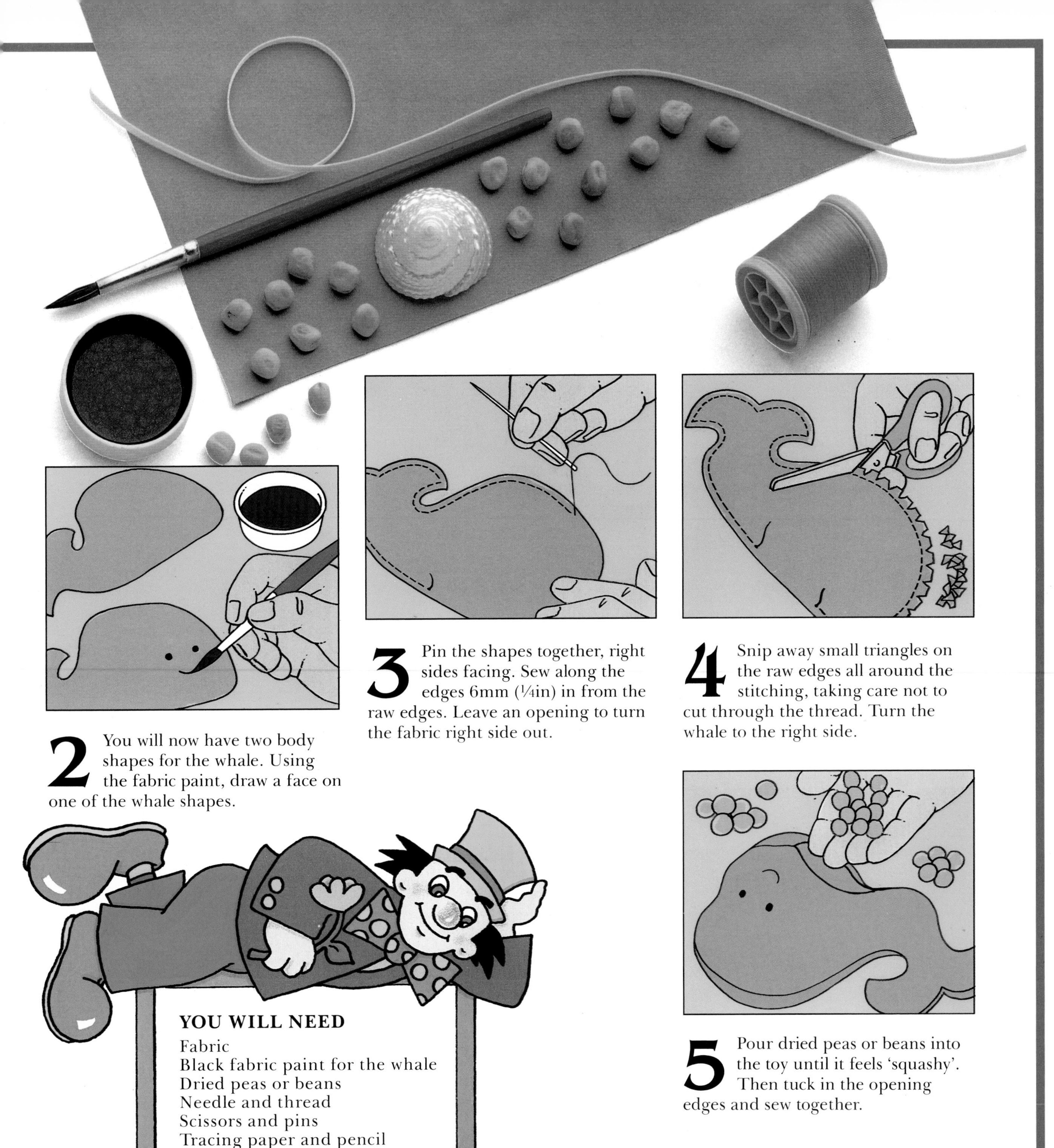

2 You will now have two body shapes for the whale. Using the fabric paint, draw a face on one of the whale shapes.

3 Pin the shapes together, right sides facing. Sew along the edges 6mm (¼in) in from the raw edges. Leave an opening to turn the fabric right side out.

4 Snip away small triangles on the raw edges all around the stitching, taking care not to cut through the thread. Turn the whale to the right side.

5 Pour dried peas or beans into the toy until it feels 'squashy'. Then tuck in the opening edges and sew together.

YOU WILL NEED

Fabric
Black fabric paint for the whale
Dried peas or beans
Needle and thread
Scissors and pins
Tracing paper and pencil
Sticky tape

DINOSAUR BADGES

These smart prehistoric monster badges are easy to make from coloured modelling clay that is baked in the oven. Choose from an ouranosaurus, a stegosaurus or a triceratops. Instead of making a badge you could glue a fridge magnet to the back.

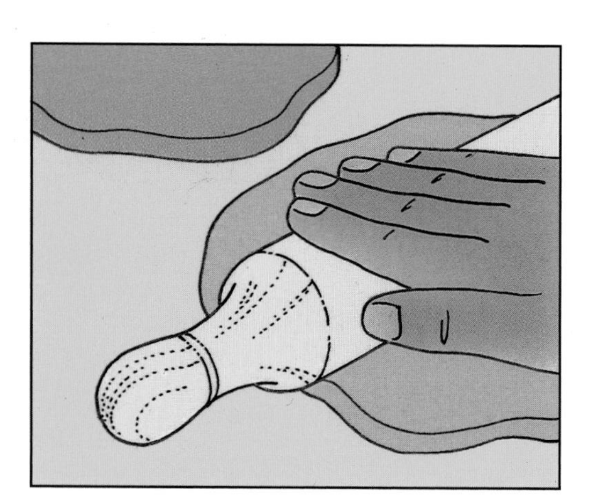

1 Roll the clay out flat to 6mm (¼in) thick. You will need one colour for the body and another for the details.

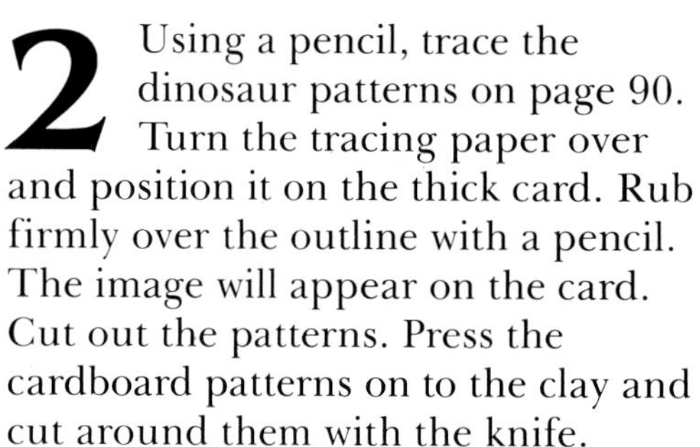

2 Using a pencil, trace the dinosaur patterns on page 90. Turn the tracing paper over and position it on the thick card. Rub firmly over the outline with a pencil. The image will appear on the card. Cut out the patterns. Press the cardboard patterns on to the clay and cut around them with the knife.

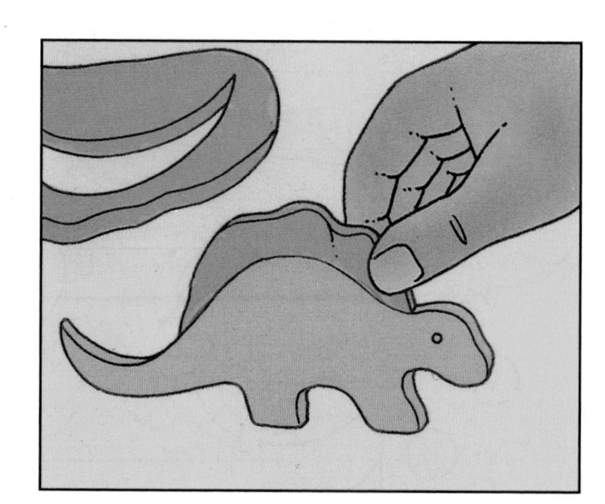

3 Remove the cardboard patterns and make an eye with a brooch pin. Press the fin on top of the ouranosaurus, squeezing it to form a wavy edge.

SAFETY TIP: *Make sure an adult helps you when using the oven.*

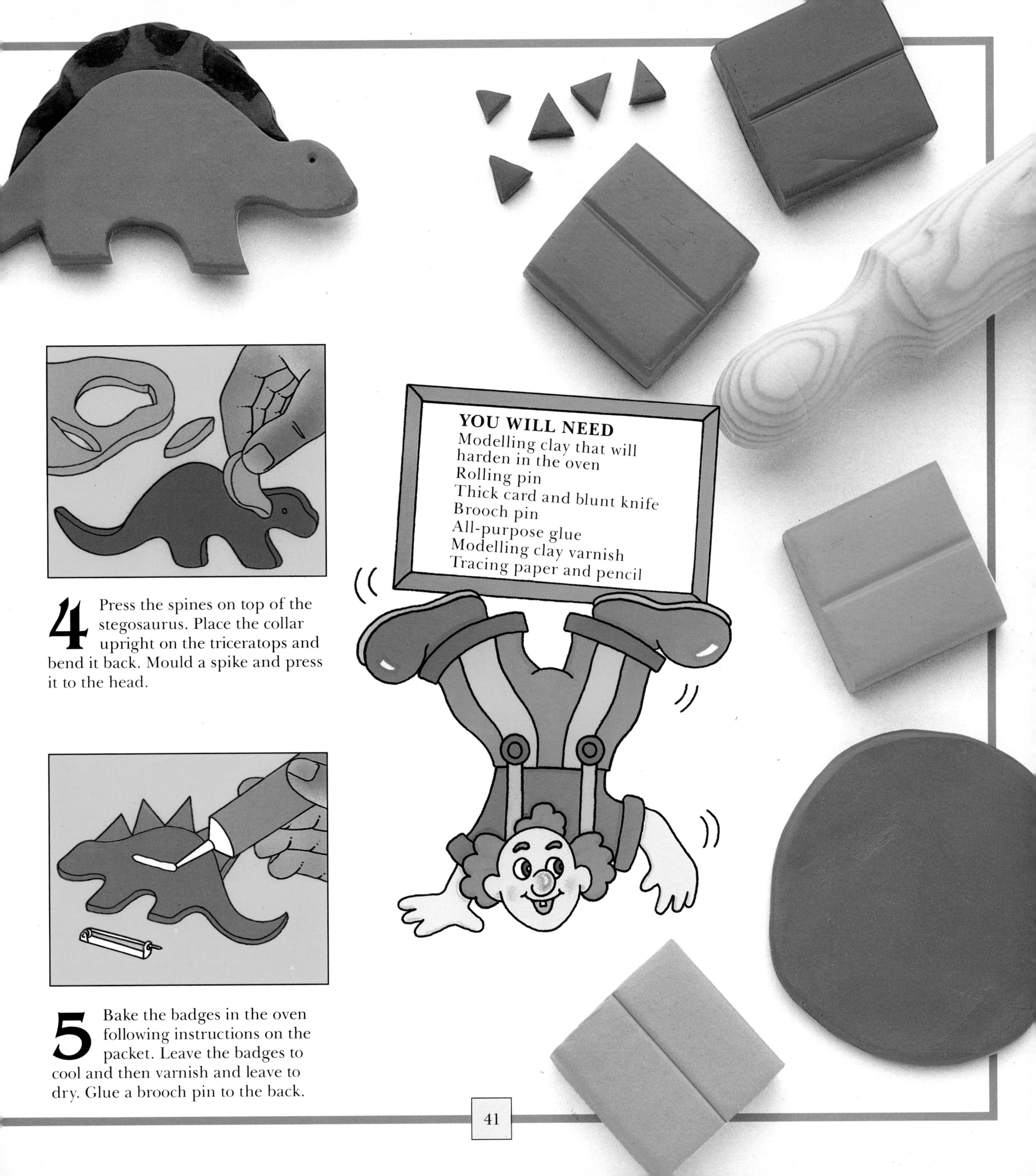

4 Press the spines on top of the stegosaurus. Place the collar upright on the triceratops and bend it back. Mould a spike and press it to the head.

5 Bake the badges in the oven following instructions on the packet. Leave the badges to cool and then varnish and leave to dry. Glue a brooch pin to the back.

ANIMAL MITTENS

These fun mittens are easy to make, warm to wear and will set your friends talking. Personalize the mittens by adding sequins, fur trims or funny animal eyes.

YOU WILL NEED

- Two squares of felt
- Fabric glue
- Wool and needle with large eye
- Trims of your choice
- Paper and pencil
- Sticky tape or pins
- Scissors

1 Place your hand on a sheet of paper and trace around it, keeping your fingers together and your thumb a bit apart. Draw a second line about 2.5cm (1in) away. Cut around the second line.

2 Lay the paper pattern, as shown here, on two layers of felt and keep in place with sticky tape or pins. Carefully cut around the pattern – you will have two hand shapes. Remove the paper pattern and repeat this step to cut out a further two hand shapes.

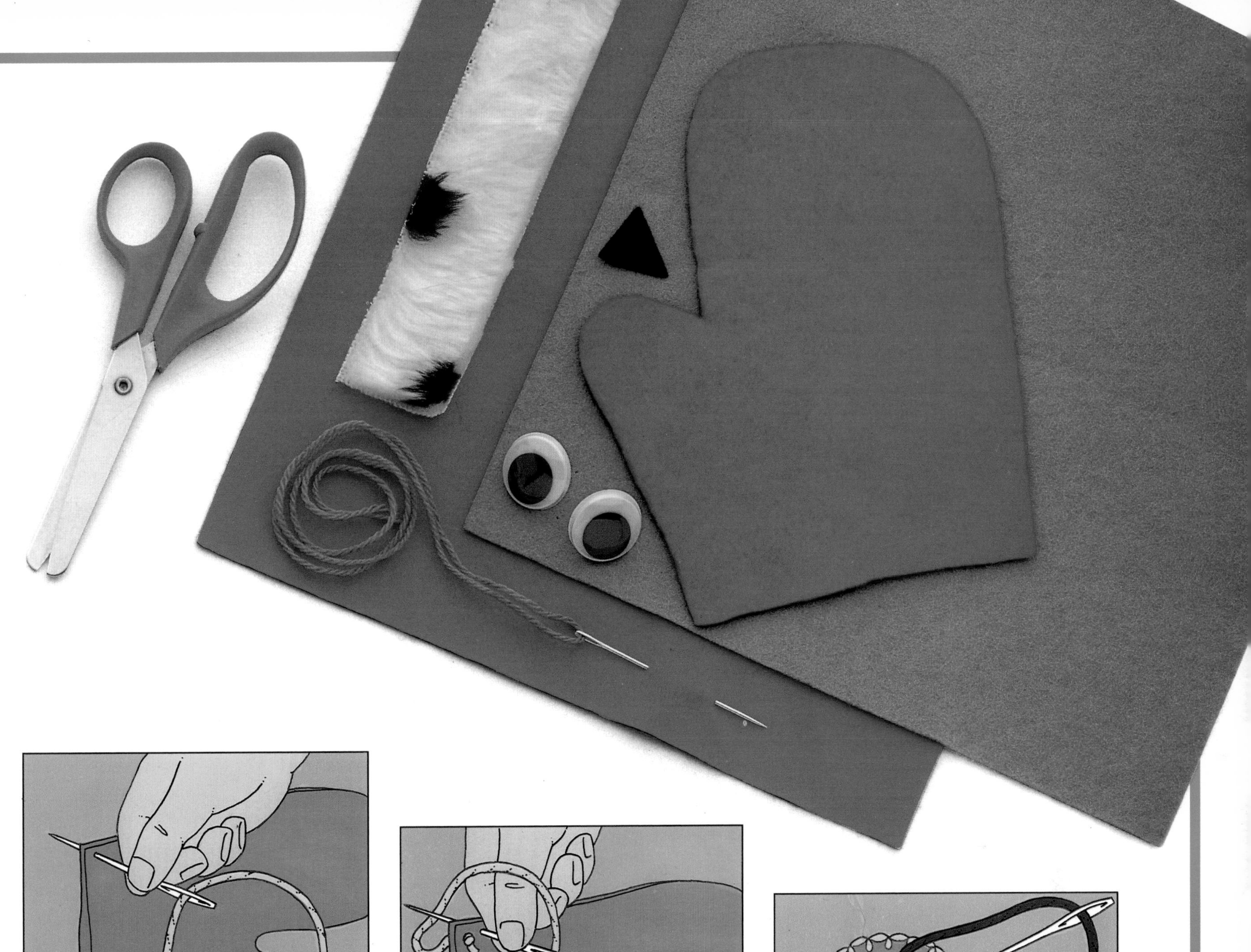

3 Thread the needle with wool and knot one end. Sew two mitten shapes together using blanket stitch. To do blanket stitch, insert the needle through both mittens from the front to the back, about 6mm (¼in) from the edge.

4 Make a second stitch 3mm (⅛in) from the first and this time take the needle through the loop that is formed, before you pull the wool firm. Repeat this method to sew all around the mitten. Do not sew across the cuff.

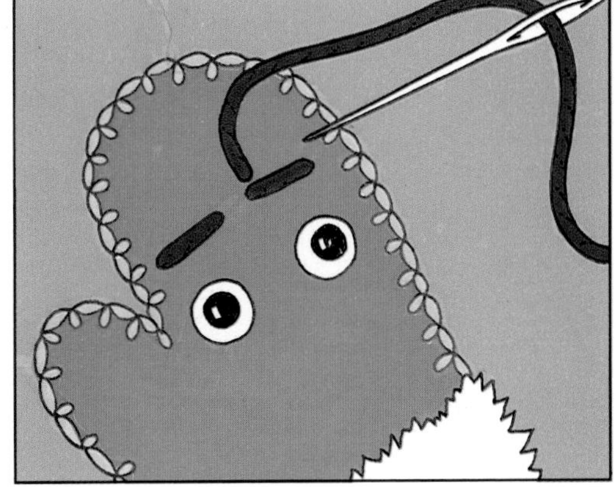

5 Decorate the mittens in any way you like; glue sequins on to them in a jazzy pattern, or stitch on fake fur and add safety eyes to make animal mittens.

These colourful tulips make great Christmas or birthday presents. Make a big bunch and arrange them in a pretty vase, or tie them together with a ribbon for a really special gift. You can also try adapting the design shown here. Use different coloured paints and cut the petals in other ways to create a wide variety of blooms.

1 Cut the egg carton into its individual sections and then cut away the corners making a point for each petal.

SAFETY TIP: *Make sure an adult helps you when using sharp scissors.*

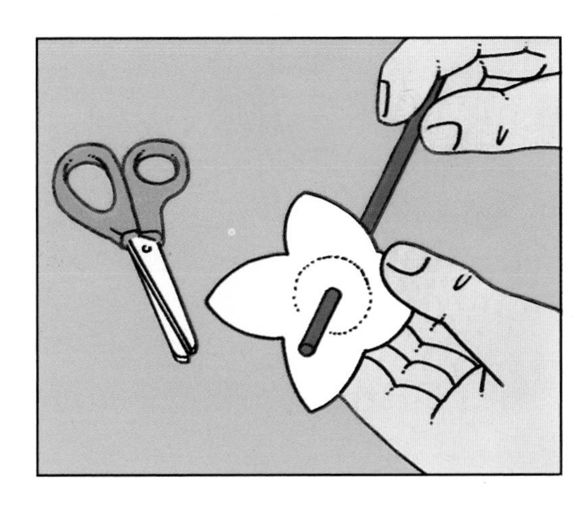

2 Ask an adult to help you pierce a hole through the base of the egg carton with the scissor points. Push the end of a garden stick up through the hole.

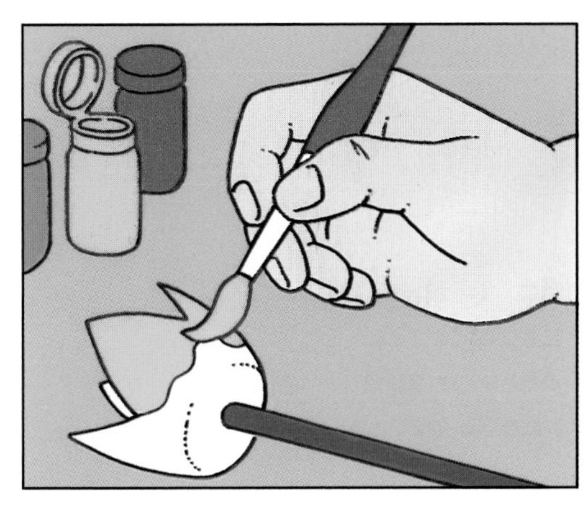

3 Now paint the tulips in bright, cheerful colours and leave to dry in a safe place.

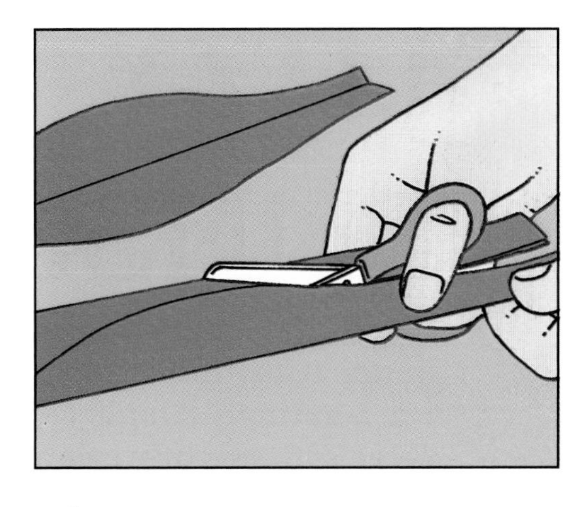

4 To make some leaves, fold strips of thin green card lengthways in half. Cut a leaf shape, as shown, and attach them to the stems with a little glue.

YOU WILL NEED

Cardboard egg carton
Garden sticks
Thin green card
Poster paints
Paintbrush
Scissors
All-purpose glue

GLITZY PLIMSOLLS

These glamorous plimsolls would look super at any disco or party and yet they are amazingly simple to do. Replace the laces with brightly coloured ones or add sparkling ribbons as we have done here.

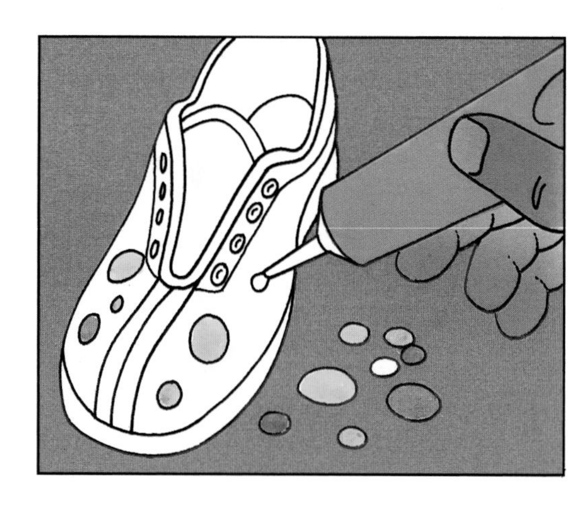

1 Glue the gemstones to the plimsolls. You can arrange the gemstones in a pattern or glue them on at random.

YOU WILL NEED

- Plain white plimsolls
- Gemstones
- Ribbon (optional)
- All-purpose glue
- Paintbrush
- Glitter pens
- Glitter paint

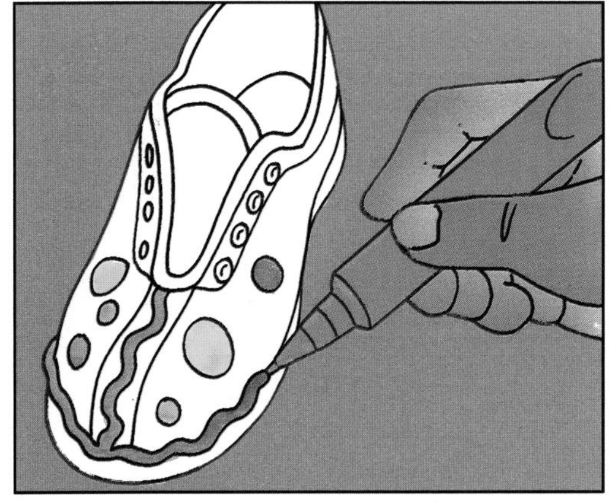

2 Decorate the plimsolls with glitter pens. Draw wavy lines along the seams then leave the glitter to dry.

3 Carefully, fill in the rest of the plimsolls with glitter paint. Leave the paint to dry then fill in any gaps with more paint.

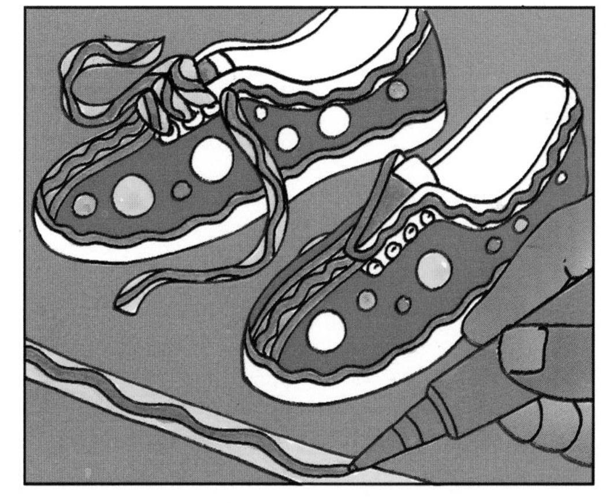

4 Cut two lengths of ribbon for the laces. Draw a wavy line on the ribbon with a glitter pen. Thread the laces through the holes when the glitter is dry.

TEDDY TRIO

These smart bears have magnets on the back so they can be attached to a metal surface, like a fridge. We show you how to make one teddy, but why not make a large family of bears in different colours and with various clothes and accessories?

1 Trace the teddy pattern on page 90 and cut out. Lay the pattern on to the yellow or honey coloured felt and carefully draw around it. Cut out the shape. Draw on the face details with a felt-tip pen.

YOU WILL NEED
Felt in different colours
Black felt-tip pen
Ribbon and string of beads
All-purpose glue
Fridge magnet
Tracing paper and pencil

2 Follow the instructions in step 1 to trace the waistcoat or skirt patterns on page 90. Cut these out from brightly coloured felt and glue to the teddy.

3 Glue the teddy to a piece of matching felt, and carefully cut around the edge. Glue a fridge magnet to the back of the teddy's head.

4 Glue a short string of beads to the girl teddy as a necklace. Tie a short length of ribbon in a knot and cut off the ends. Glue this to the boy teddy as a bow-tie.

Clown Collage

Collect oddments of fabric, wool, buttons and beads to make this jolly clown collage. Glue a picture hanger to the back and you can hang it on your bedroom door as a name plaque.

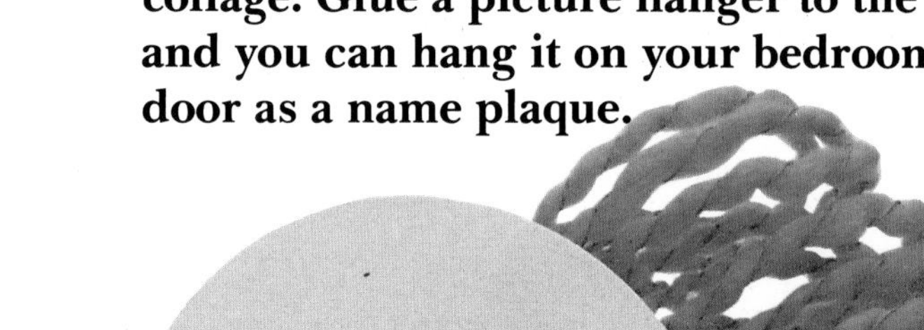

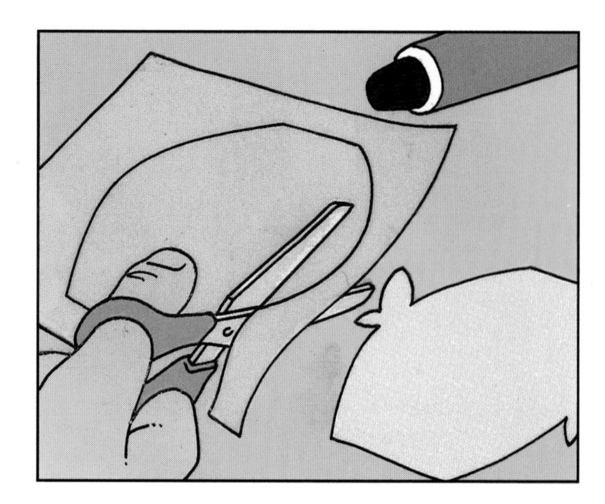

1 Using a pencil, trace the clown pattern on page 91. Turn the tracing over and hold it in position on the pink card. Rub firmly over the outline with a pencil. The clown pattern will appear on the card. Cut out. Lay this shape on to the fabric and draw around it. Cut out the fabric body, but do not cut out the hands. Glue the fabric on to the card.

2 Cut out a circle of white card 8cm (3¼in) in diameter for the head. Cut a strip of crêpe paper and glue one long edge behind the head scrunching it around the 'neck' to fit.

YOU WILL NEED
Pink and white card
Printed fabric, red felt, wool, crêpe paper, red felt-tip pen, 2 buttons, a bead and 2 pompons
Picture hanger
All-purpose glue and scissors
Tracing paper and pencil

3 Glue a bead to the head as a nose and two buttons for the eyes. Draw a mouth with a felt-tip pen. Glue loops of wool to the head for the hair.

4 Glue the head to the body. Trace the shoe patterns on page 91 and cut out. Pin the tracings on to the red felt and cut out two shoes. Glue them to the body and glue a pompon to each shoe.

5 Bend the cardboard hands upwards. Write your name on a strip of paper – 2.5cm (1in) longer than the width of the body – and glue the ends to the hands. The name strip will curve out nicely from the body.

FINGER PUPPETS

Finger puppets can be a real handful – especially if you make a complete set. Make the puppets to look like your favourite animals or fairy-tale characters. They also make ideal presents for younger brothers and sisters.

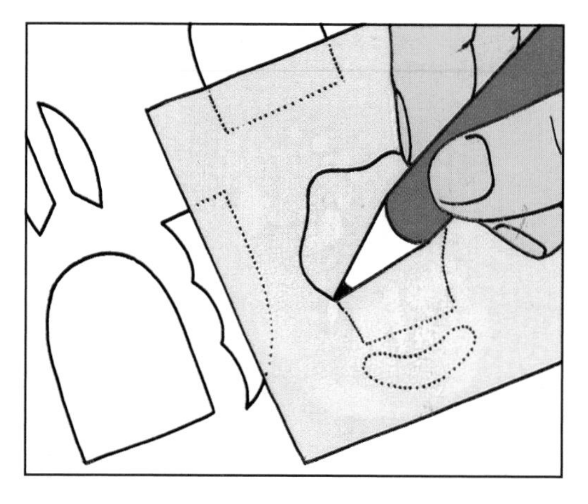

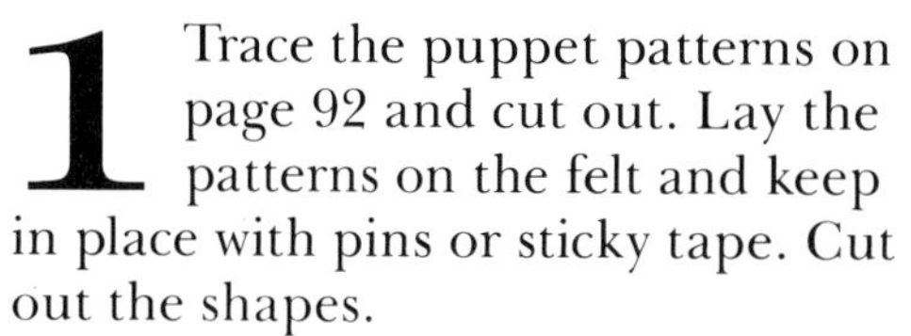

1 Trace the puppet patterns on page 92 and cut out. Lay the patterns on the felt and keep in place with pins or sticky tape. Cut out the shapes.

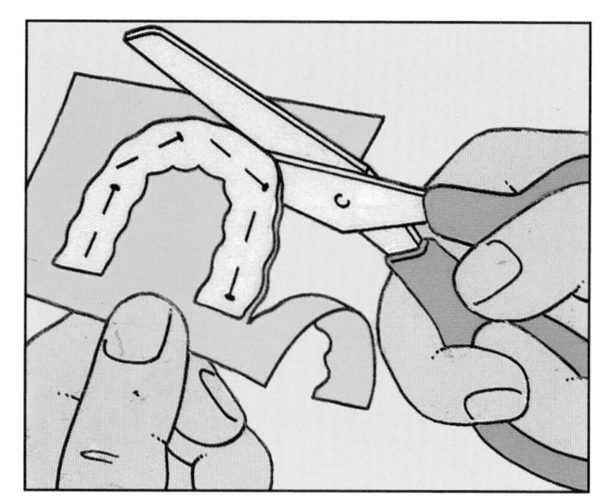

2 Follow the instructions in step 1 to trace the main features, like the princess's hair, from the patterns on page 92. Extra features, like noses or whiskers, can be cut directly from scraps of felt.

3 If using them, paint on features using the fabric paints. Leave the paint to dry.

4 Use glue to attach features like hair and hats. Stitch whiskers on at this stage.

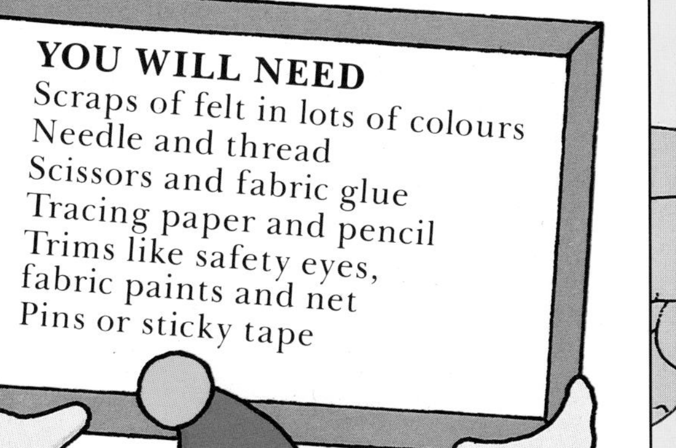

YOU WILL NEED
Scraps of felt in lots of colours
Needle and thread
Scissors and fabric glue
Tracing paper and pencil
Trims like safety eyes, fabric paints and net
Pins or sticky tape

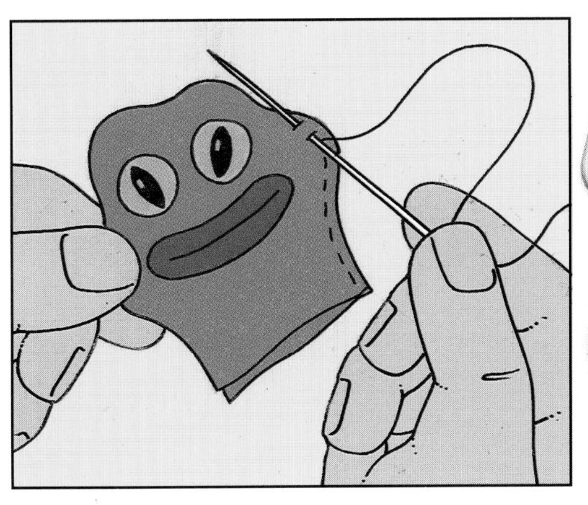

5 Sew up the sides of the puppet – taking care not to sew across the base.

PAPIER MÂCHÉ BOWLS

Turn old newspapers into pretty bowls using a method known as papier mâché. The bowls can be painted in bright colours to match your room. They also make ideal Christmas or birthday gifts.

1 Cover the work area with lots of spare newspaper. Turn the mug upside-down and balance the bowl on top of it. Tear or cut some newspaper into strips.

YOU WILL NEED
Newspaper and PVA glue
Old glass or plastic bowl
Mug
Old dish or cup
Petroleum jelly
Old paintbrush
Poster paints and brushes
Scissors

2 Cover the bowl with a thick coat of petroleum jelly – this stops the papier mâché from sticking later. Pour some glue into an old dish and thin it with water.

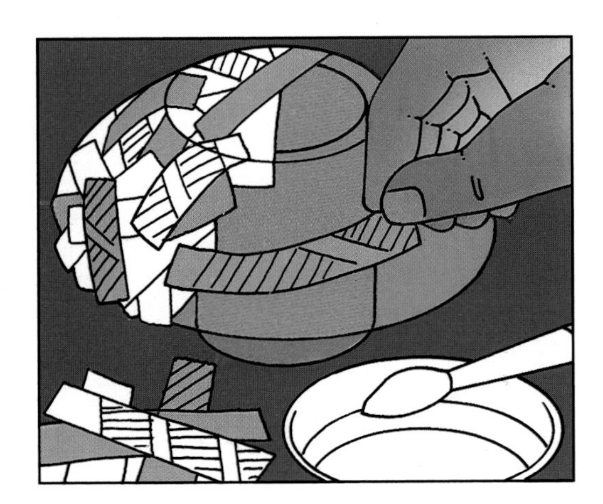

3 Using the old paintbrush, coat the paper strips with glue and lay them over the bowl, one at a time. When the bowl is covered with paper strips, paint glue all over them.

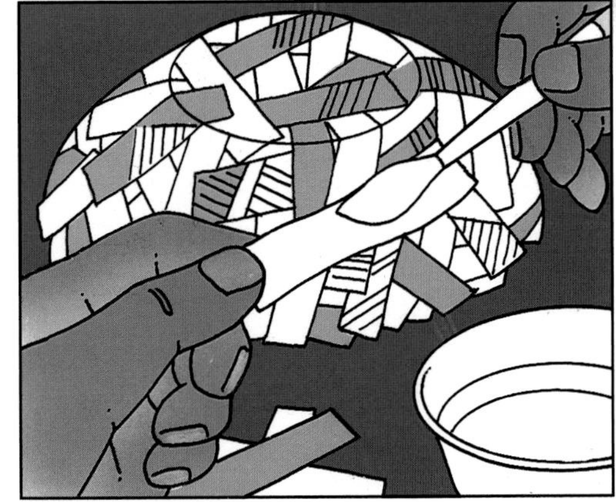

4 Repeat step 3 at least eight times, making sure you overlap the strips each time. Leave the paper bowl to dry in a warm spot for a few days.

5 When the bowl is dry, gently ease it off the glass bowl and trim any rough edges with scissors. Paint the bowl in a bright colour or a cheerful pattern.

PAPER JEWELLERY

Deck yourself out in this stylish jewellery – it is made from rolled up paper and coloured wooden beads, threaded on wool. The same technique can be used to make matching earrings, pendants, brooches or bangles.

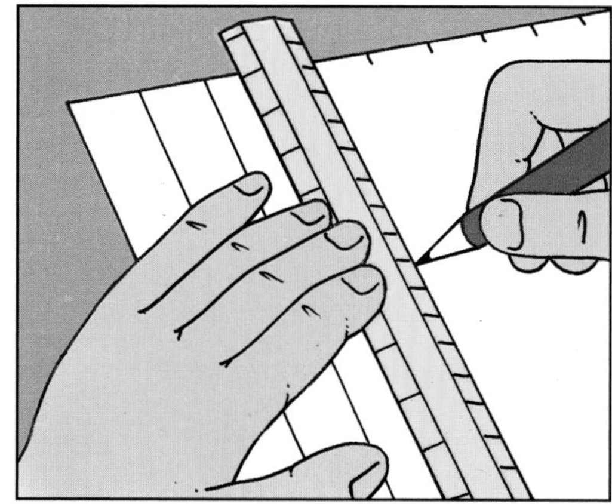

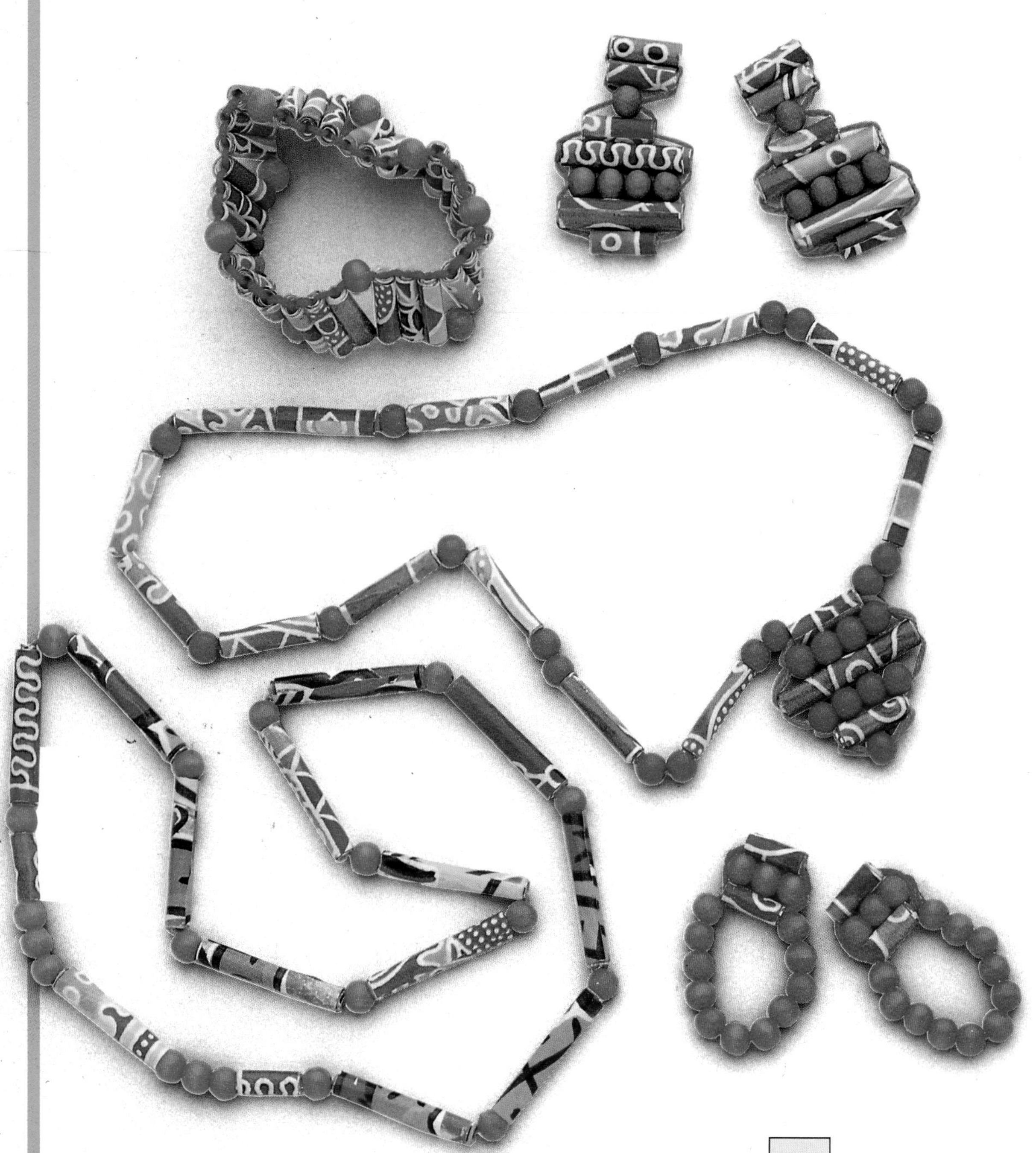

1 To make the paper beads, use the ruler and pencil to draw strips on the back of the paper. The strips should be about 20cm (8in) long and as wide as you want the bead to be – about 2.5cm (1in) is a good size. Cut out the strips.

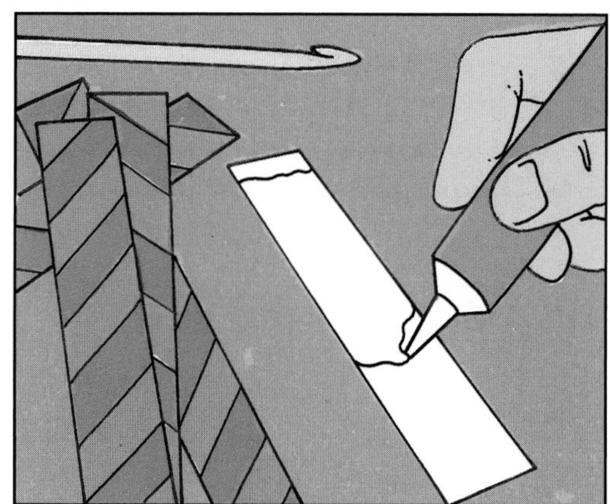

2 Dab glue over the back of one strip, leaving about 6mm (¼in) at one end. Position the knitting needle or crochet hook on the unglued end of the paper strip. Carefully roll the strip around the needle or hook to make the bead.

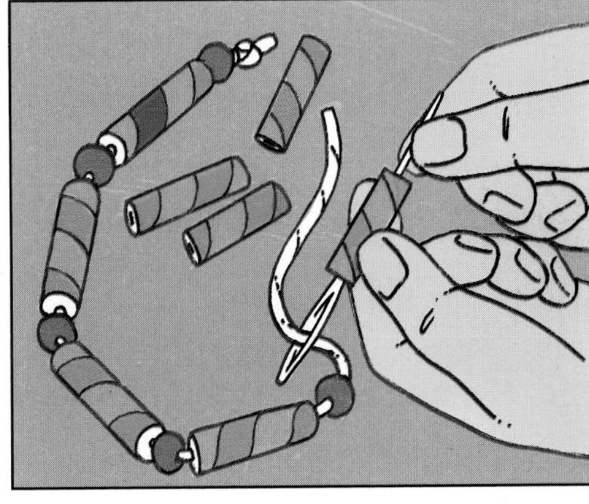

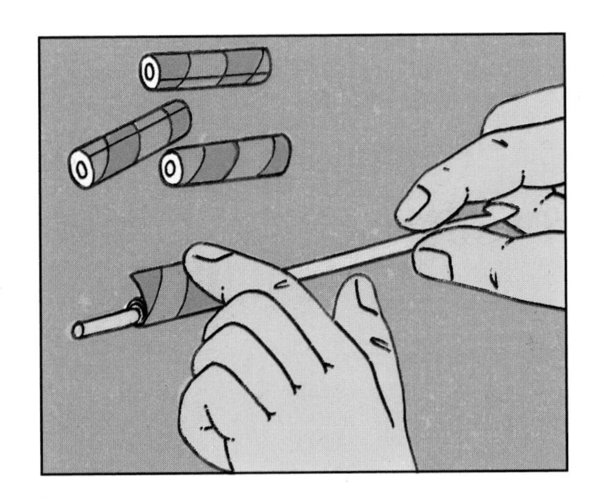

3 Make sure the end of the strip is stuck down well. Slip the paper bead off the needle. Repeat step 3 to make as many beads as you need for a necklace or bracelet.

4 For a string of beads, thread the needle with wool and tie a knot in one end. Thread the beads on to the wool, then knot the ends of the wool together making sure that it is long enough to go over your head or hand.

5 To make a row of vertical beads, like the bracelet shown here, thread a needle on to each end of the length of wool. Thread the first bead to the centre of the wool. Push one needle through the next bead. Push the other needle through the same bead in the opposite way. Repeat with the other beads.

YOU WILL NEED
Magazine pages or gift wrap
Glue
Wool
Coloured wooden beads
Ruler and pencil
Scissors
Crochet hook or knitting needle
Blunt ended needle

WOVEN BAGS

Weaving is a method used to make fabrics. You can use almost any material, from wool to strips of fabric. Ribbon and wool make a good combination because they give quick results and look great!

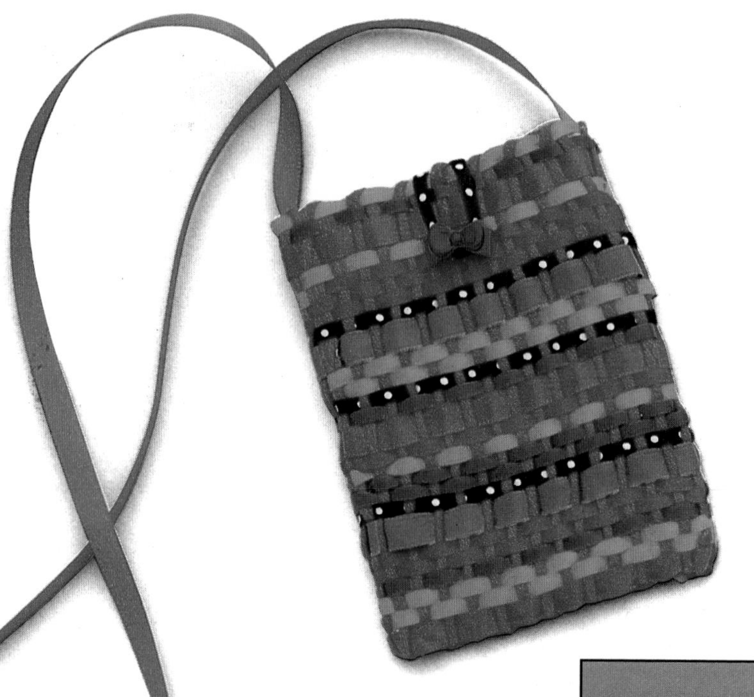

1 Draw a rectangle, twice as big as you want the bag to be, on to the card; cut out. Mark small lines 6mm (¼in) apart along both short edges. Cut into the card at each mark.

2 Slip the wool into the first notch and tie it in place. Take the wool down into the notch at the opposite end of the card, then across at the back and bring it through the next notch.

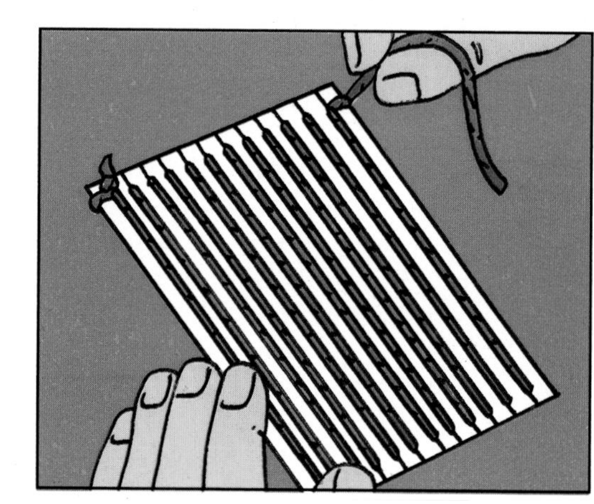

3 Take the wool back up to the opposite side and repeat step 2 to thread the card with wool. In weaving, these vertical lengths of yarn are called the warp.

SAFETY TIP: *Make sure an adult helps you when using the iron.*

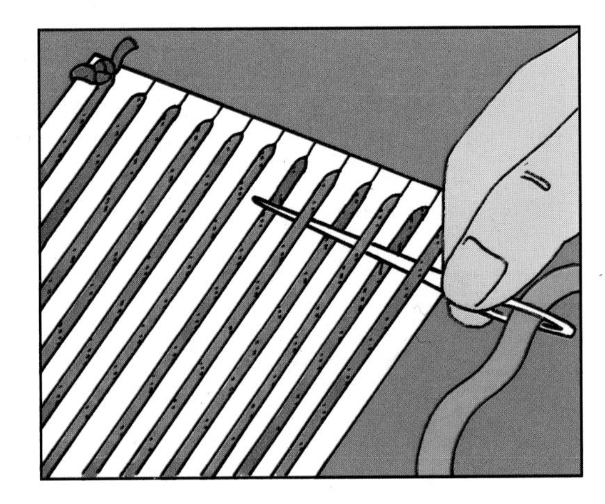

4 Cut the ribbon into lengths the same width as the card plus 5cm (2in). Thread the needle with ribbon and weave it in and out across the card, taking it under one strand of wool and over the next.

YOU WILL NEED

Large, firm piece of card
Scissors
Ruler and pencil
Wool
Lots of colourful ribbons
Iron-on felt
Button (optional)
Blunt needle with large eye

5 Take the next piece of ribbon over the threads in the opposite way. If you started with the first length of ribbon going over the wool, take it under this time. Repeat steps 4 and 5 until the weaving is complete.

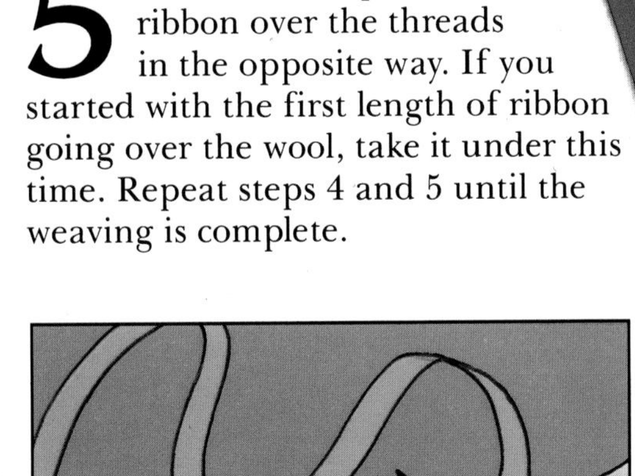

6 To make the bag, gently ease the weaving off the card. Ask an adult to help you iron the felt to the back of the weaving, then fold in half and sew up the sides. Add a ribbon handle.

GLIDERS

Have fun making these gliders and hours more fun flying them. They are made from card and weighted to ensure that they fly really well. So, don't stop at one – make a whole squadron!

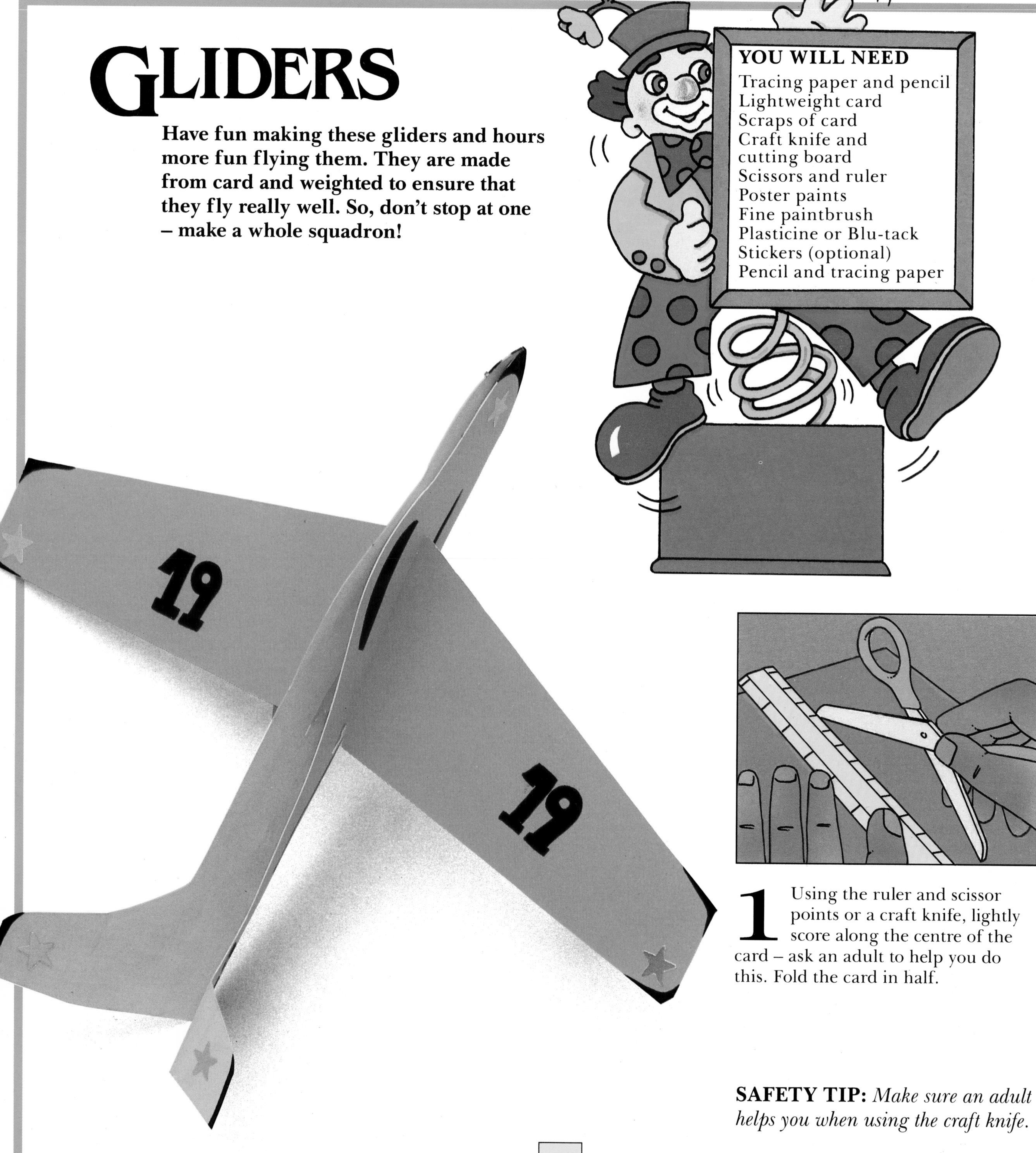

YOU WILL NEED
Tracing paper and pencil
Lightweight card
Scraps of card
Craft knife and cutting board
Scissors and ruler
Poster paints
Fine paintbrush
Plasticine or Blu-tack
Stickers (optional)
Pencil and tracing paper

1 Using the ruler and scissor points or a craft knife, lightly score along the centre of the card – ask an adult to help you do this. Fold the card in half.

SAFETY TIP: *Make sure an adult helps you when using the craft knife.*

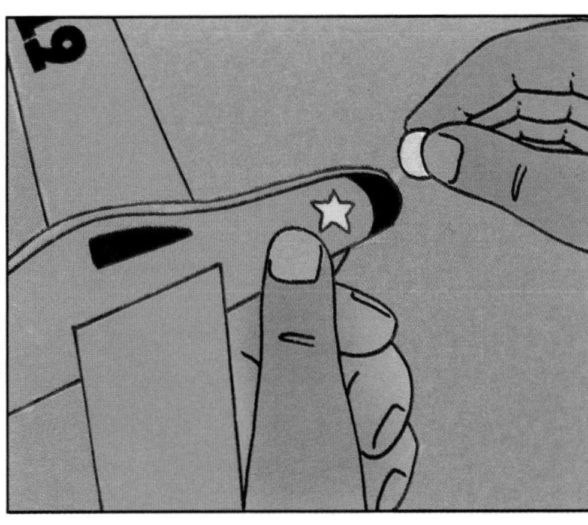

4 Push the wings into the plane slit. Bend down the tail of the plane along the line marked on the pattern. Weight the nose with a small piece of Plasticine or Blu-tack.

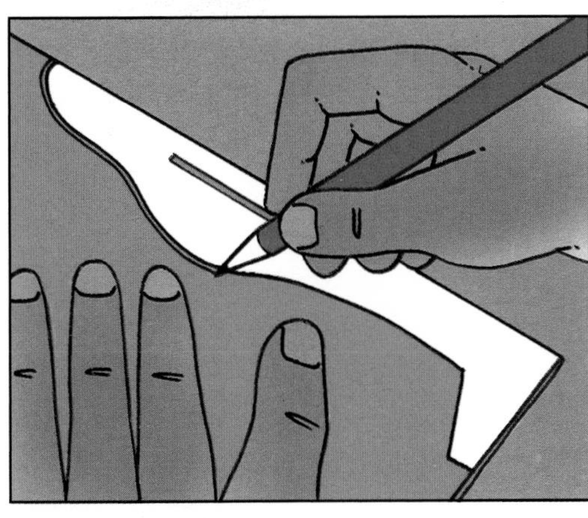

2 Using a pencil, trace the plane body pattern on page 93. Turn the tracing over and lay it against the fold of the card as shown. Rub firmly over the outline with a pencil. The pattern will appear on the card. Cut out the shape. Cut out the wing slits with a craft knife.

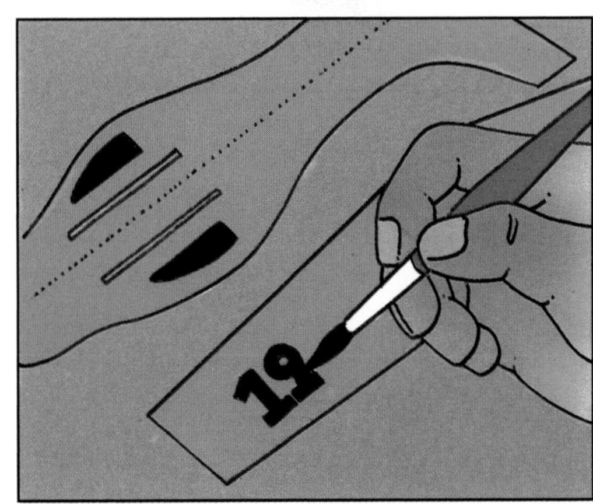

3 Trace the wing pattern following the instructions in step 2. Cut the wings from a single layer of card. Paint the plane however you like. Add stickers when the paint is dry.

CARDBOARD BADGES

Pin these badges on to your jacket or sweater to give it a unique look. Copy the crazy animal shapes here or make your own. The badges can be almost any shape, and decorated in any way you choose.

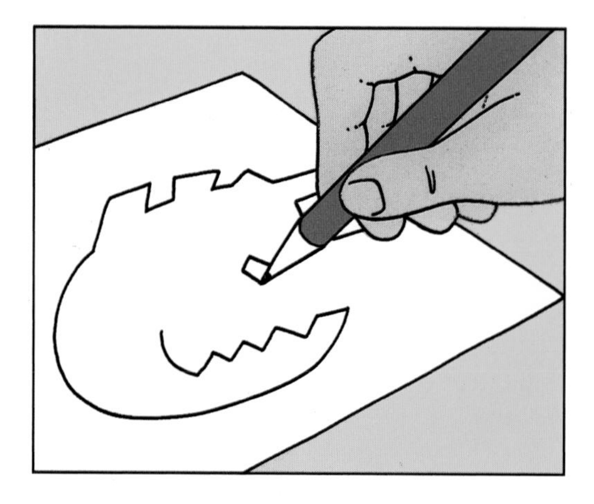

1 Using a pencil, trace one of the patterns on page 92. Or try drawing your own animal shapes on scrap paper.

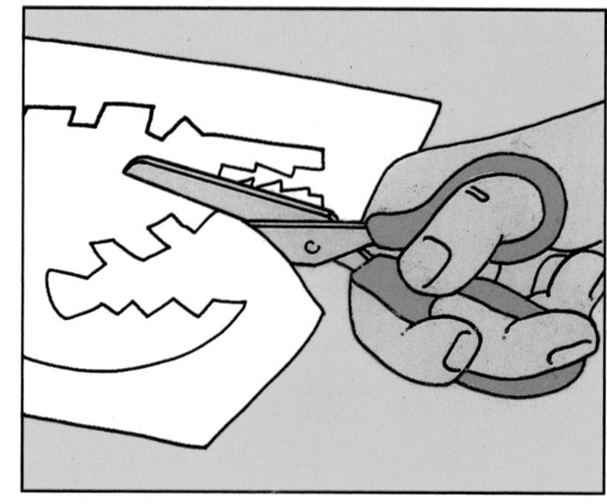

2 Turn the tracing over and hold it in position on the card. Rub firmly over the outline with a pencil. The shape will appear on the card. Cut out the card shape using the scissors.

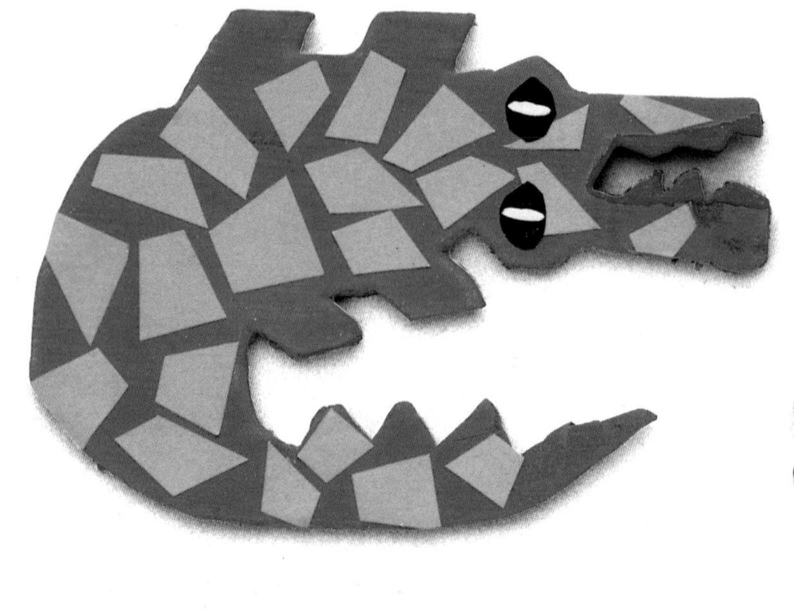

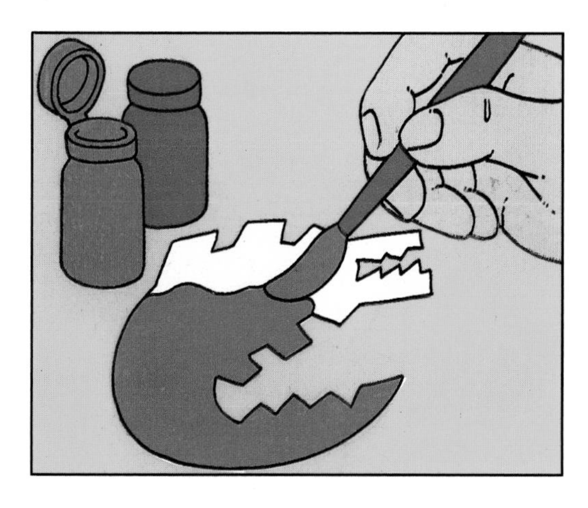

3 Paint your badge a bright colour. To get a strong colour, let the first coat dry and paint the shape a second time. Leave the paint to dry.

4 Decorate the badge with coloured stickers. Use the stickers as they are or cut them into different shapes. Use the fine paintbrush to paint details, like eyes.

5 When the badge is complete, turn it over and tape a safety pin to the back. Pin it to your favourite clothes.

BASEBALL CAP

Use glitter pens, sparkling sequins and gemstones to decorate clothes and accessories. The range of things that can be decorated is limitless, from your socks or T-shirts to a fashionable baseball cap.

YOU WILL NEED
A selection of sequins and coloured gems
All-purpose glue
Glitter pens or fabric paints
A white cap to decorate

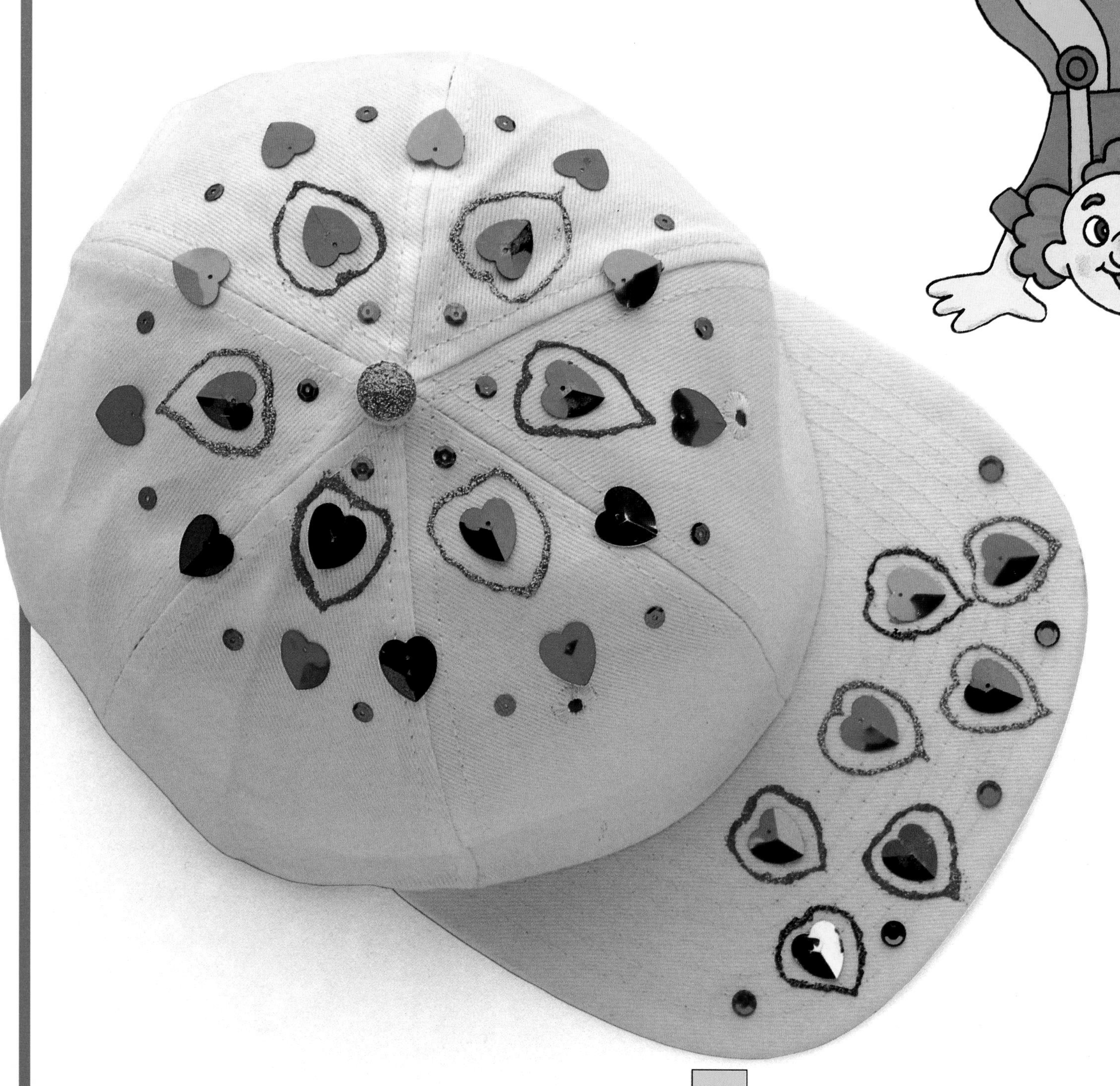

1 Plan your design on a piece of white paper, moving the sequins and gemstones around until you are happy with the pattern they form.

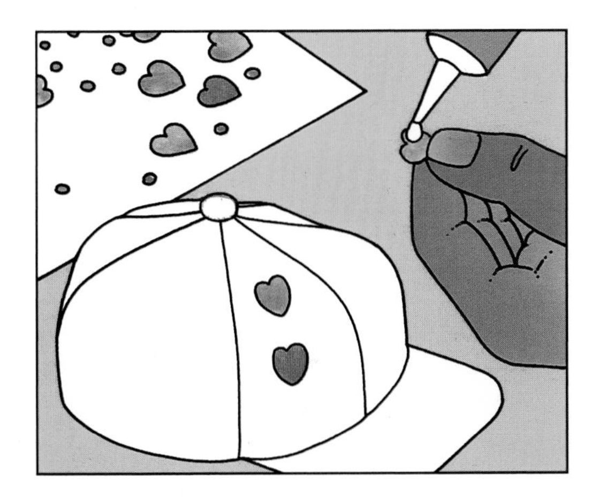

2 Dab a small amount of glue on to the back of the sequin or stone and stick it to the cap. Repeat until all the gems are in place.

3 Practise using the fabric paints or glitter pens on a scrap of paper. Apply a gentle, even pressure on the tubes to draw a line. If you squeeze too hard the paint will come out in blobs.

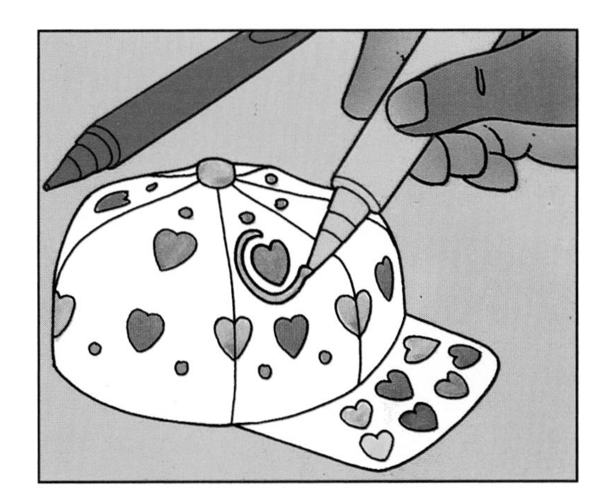

4 When you are happy with your paint technique, draw designs on the cap. Take extra care as the marks will be permanent. Follow the manufacturer's instructions to set the paint or pens so that they don't smudge. Ask an adult to help if you are uncertain how to do this.

SLITHERING SNAKE

Pretend this snake is real – it will wriggle along if it is pulled over a smooth surface, like a table or the floor. It is made from polystyrene packing, which often comes around shop-bought items.

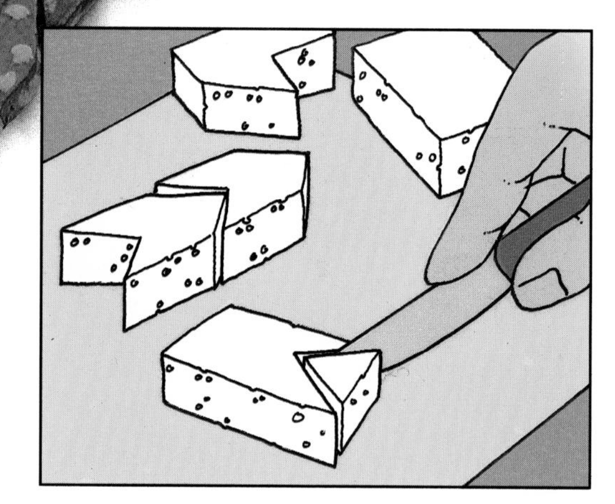

2 With the sharp knife, trim one end of the rectangles into a point. Trim the other end into a wide 'V' shape. Make sure that the pieces fit together, so that when the point sits into the 'V' the snake can move from side to side. Cut a 'V' into the base of the head. Paint the shapes and leave to dry.

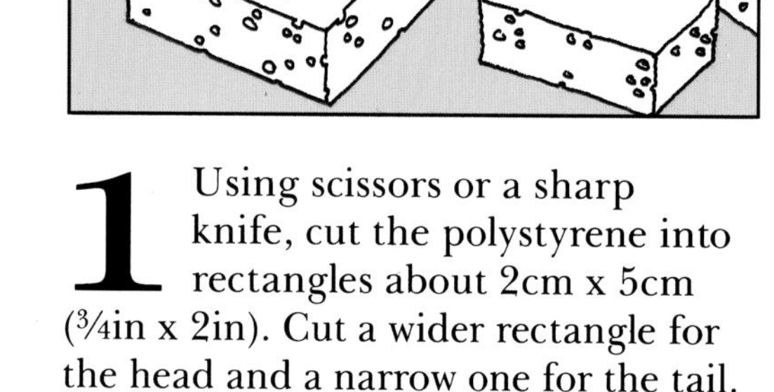

1 Using scissors or a sharp knife, cut the polystyrene into rectangles about 2cm x 5cm (¾in x 2in). Cut a wider rectangle for the head and a narrow one for the tail.

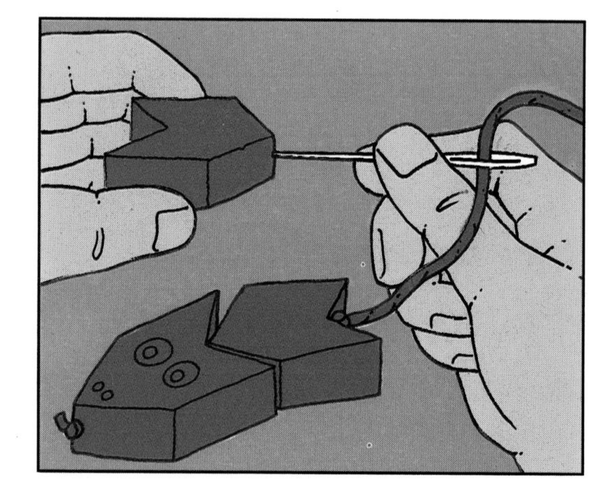

3 Thread the needle with wool and knot the end. Push the needle through the snake's head as shown. Tie a knot and thread the next shape on. Repeat until all the shapes are threaded, tying a knot between each one.

SAFETY TIP: *Make sure an adult helps you when using the sharp knife.*

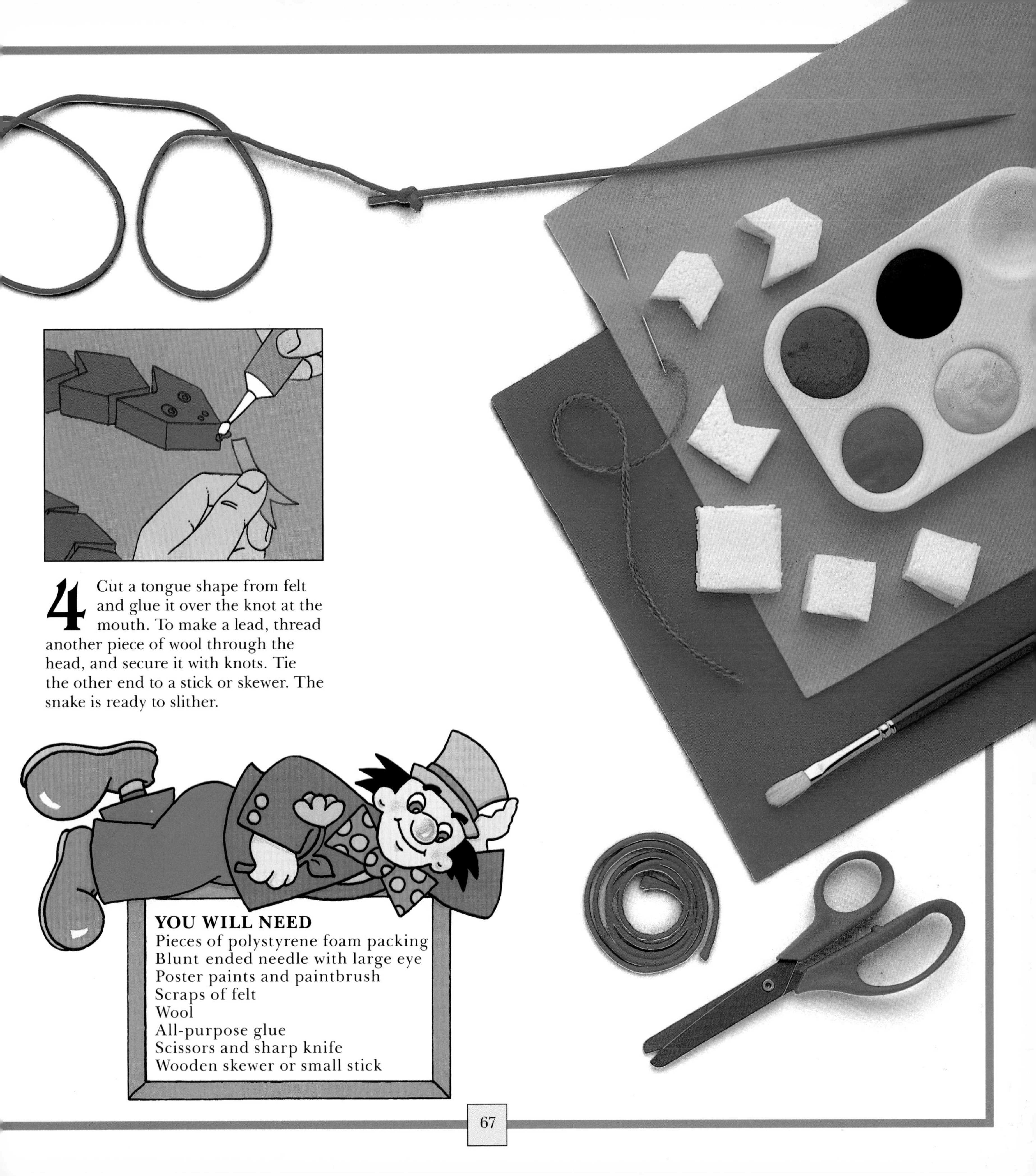

4 Cut a tongue shape from felt and glue it over the knot at the mouth. To make a lead, thread another piece of wool through the head, and secure it with knots. Tie the other end to a stick or skewer. The snake is ready to slither.

YOU WILL NEED
Pieces of polystyrene foam packing
Blunt ended needle with large eye
Poster paints and paintbrush
Scraps of felt
Wool
All-purpose glue
Scissors and sharp knife
Wooden skewer or small stick

BREAKFAST KEY-RINGS

Surprise your friends and keep your keys safe at the same time, with these unusual key-rings made from coloured modelling clay. Bake and varnish the clay following the instructions on the packet. Fit the key-ring only when the varnish has dried.

YOU WILL NEED

- Modelling clay that will harden in the oven
- Modelling clay varnish
- Old key-rings
- Plastic rolling pin or plastic mug
- Blunt knife
- Baking tray

1 To make the fried egg, roll white clay to 6mm (¼in) thick. Trim into a fried egg shape. Roll yellow clay into a flat ball; press into the white clay. Pierce a hole for the key-ring.

2 For the baked beans on toast, roll brown clay to about 6mm (¼in) thick and trim it into a triangle. Make 'sauce' from thin strips of red clay. Lay the strips on to the white triangle.

3 Roll small pieces of brown clay into balls and gently push them on to the 'sauce' to look like beans. Pierce a small hole in the corner of the white triangle.

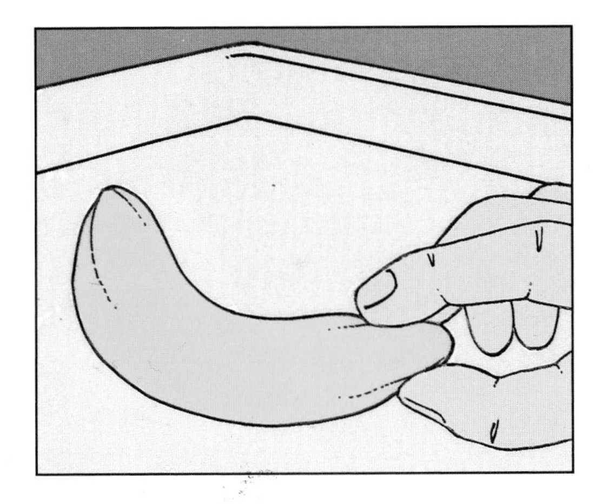

4 To make the banana, roll pale yellow clay into a thick sausage. Flatten one side of the sausage shape by pressing it on to the baking tray. Curve it into a banana shape, pinching the ends into points.

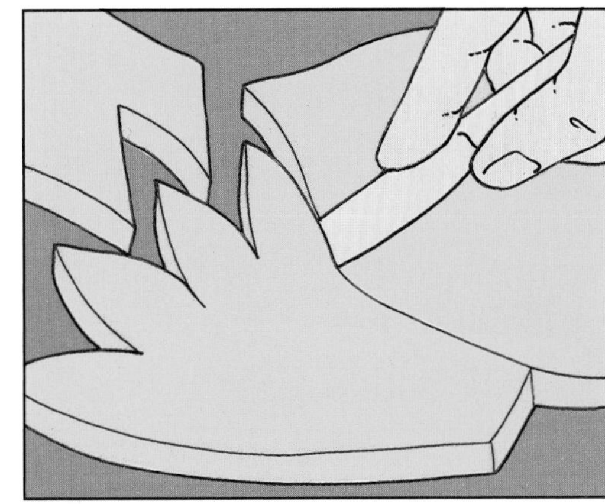

5 Roll dark yellow clay to about 6mm (¼in) thick and cut the banana 'skin' as shown above. Lay the skin on to the 'banana', then gently peel back the top sections. Press small strips and dots of brown clay into the skin. Pierce a small hole in the top of the banana. Bake the shapes following the instructions on the packet.

SAFETY TIP: *Make sure an adult helps you when using the oven.*

POTATO PRINTS

Potatoes make great printing blocks as they can be used over and over again to print envelopes, cards and wrapping paper. You can copy the patterns shown here, or design your own motifs.

SAFETY TIP: *Make sure an adult helps you when using the sharp knife.*

YOU WILL NEED

Paper or envelopes to print
Large to medium-sized potatoes
Felt-tip pen
Sharp knife
Paintbrush
Poster paints
Tracing paper and pencil
Card and scissors

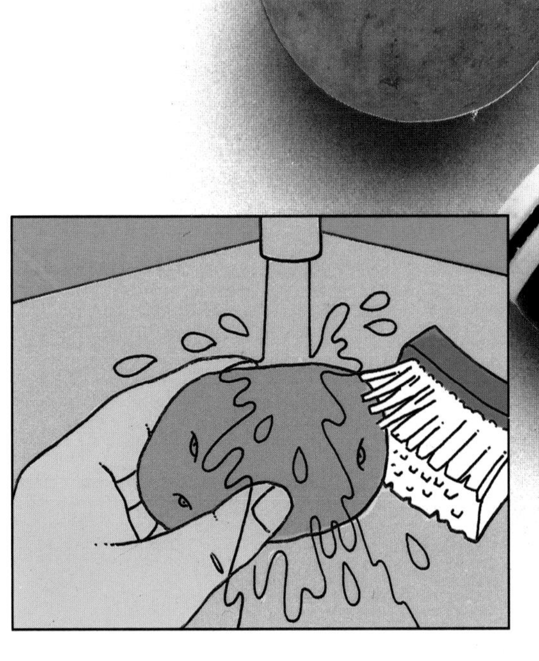

1 Wash the potatoes to remove the dirt on the outside of the skin and leave them to dry. When they are dry, ask an adult to help you cut them in half.

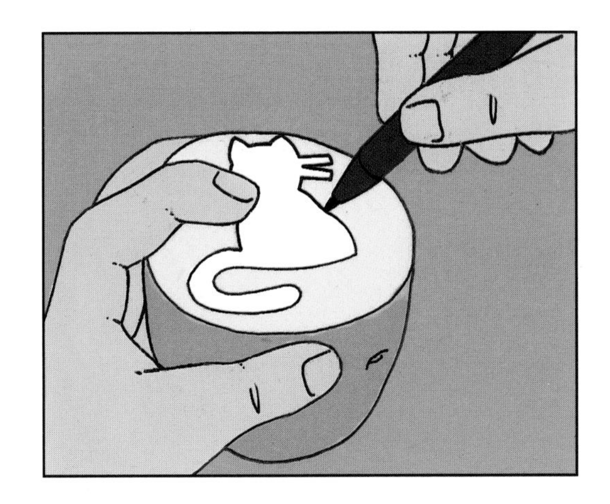

2 Using a pencil, trace one of the patterns on page 93, or design your own motif. Turn the tracing over and hold it in position on the card. Rub firmly over the outline with a pencil. The pattern will appear on the card. Cut the pattern out and place on the potato. Draw carefully round the shape with the pen.

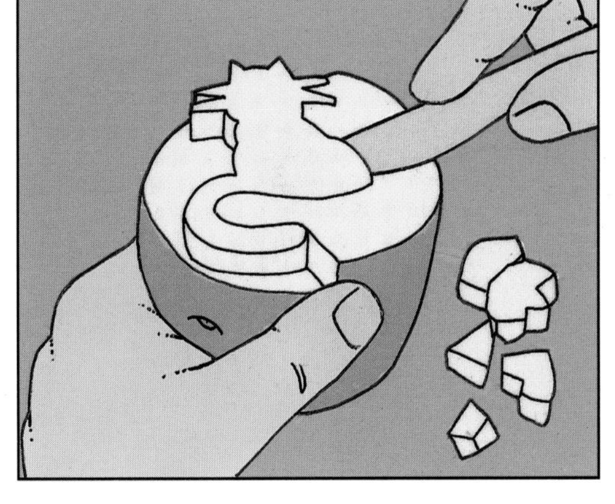

3 Using the sharp knife, cut away a thin layer of potato around the shape so that it stands out. Ask an adult to help you do this.

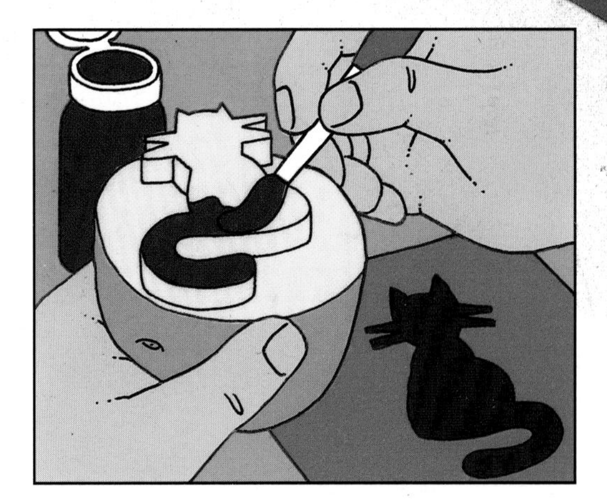

4 Coat the raised shape with paint and press it down on to the paper or envelopes. Repeat to print another shape. To print a second colour, use another potato half or wipe off the first colour. When the prints are dry you can add painted features like eyes.

HIP BELTS

Jazz up your clothes with a fun belt, made in a crazy daisy pattern, or ultra fashionable tartan. The belts can be adjusted in size by adding or subtracting one or more shapes. Here, they have been designed to be worn around your hips in true 1960s style.

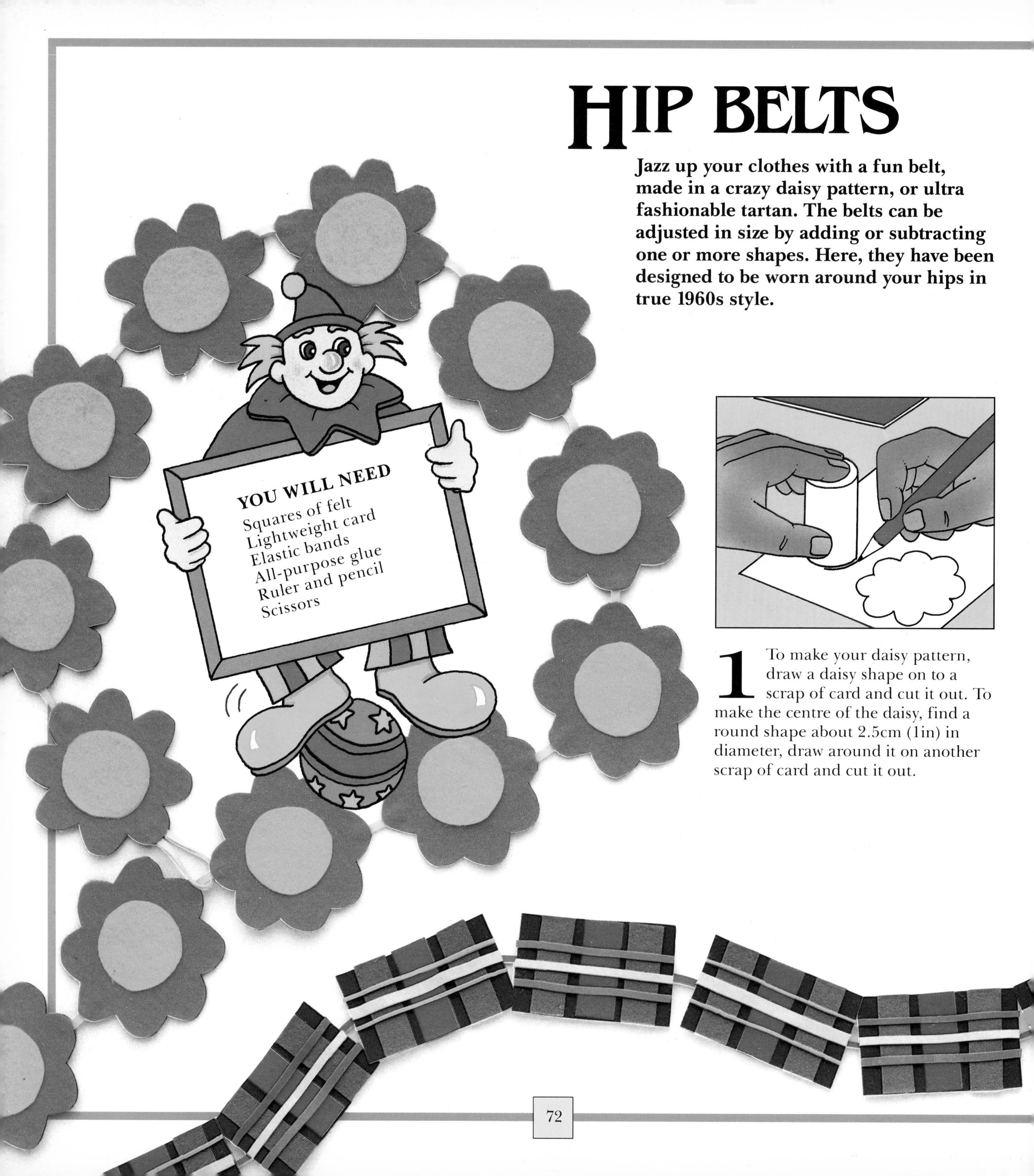

1 To make your daisy pattern, draw a daisy shape on to a scrap of card and cut it out. To make the centre of the daisy, find a round shape about 2.5cm (1in) in diameter, draw around it on another scrap of card and cut it out.

2 Coat a sheet of card with glue and stick the felt squares on to it. Turn the sheet over so that the card side is facing you. Draw around the daisy shape 10 times and the circle 10 times. Cut out the shapes.

3 Glue the circles to the centres of the daisies. Cut elastic bands into pieces 2.5cm (1in) long and glue them to the back of the daisies. Glue an elastic loop to the end daisy.

4 Cut more daisy shapes just from felt and glue them on to the back of the card shapes, covering the ends of the elastic bands.

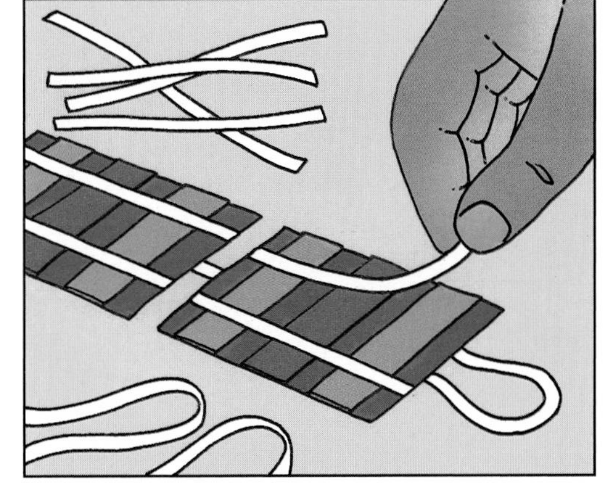

5 Make the tartan belt in a similar way. Start with rectangles of felt and glue extra strips of felt on top. Glue wide elastic bands across the felt strips. Make up the tartan belt in the same way as before.

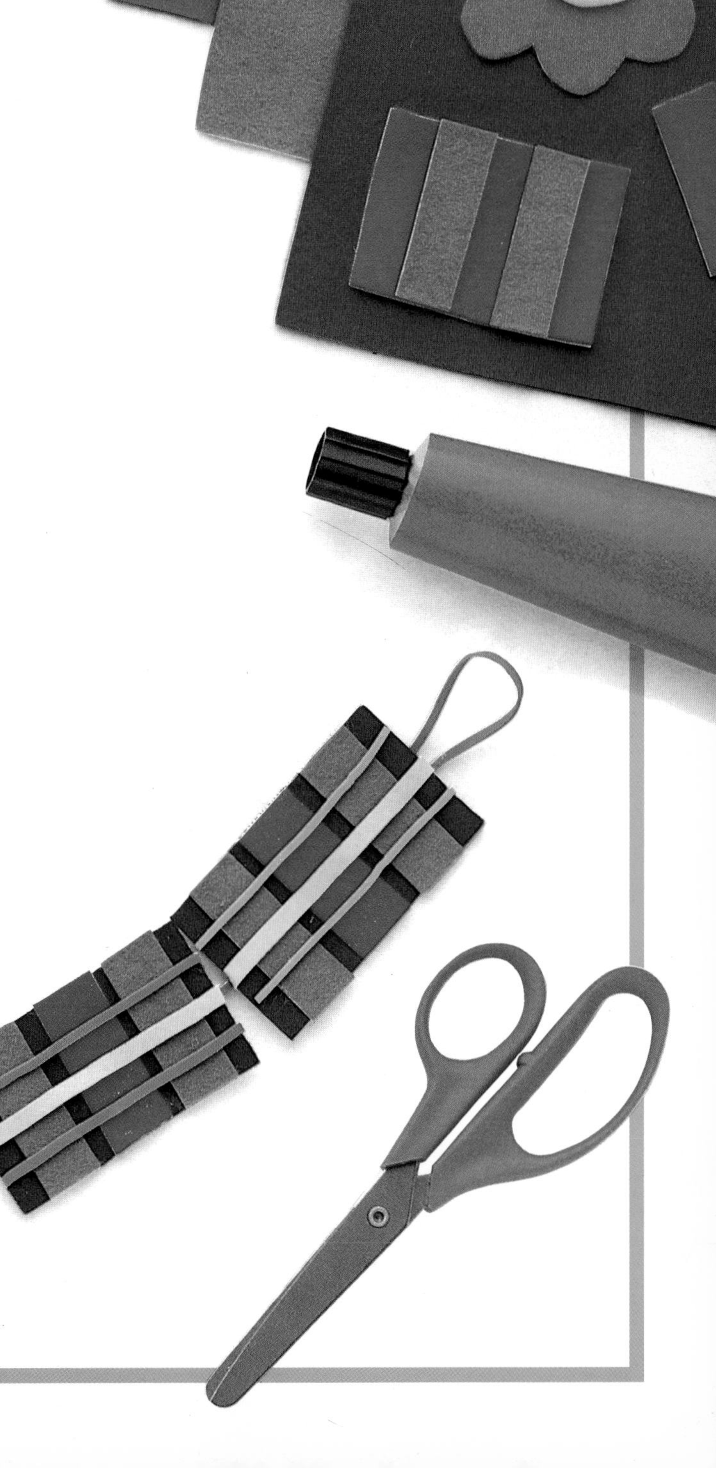

CONCERTINA CATS

Make these stripy cats as a personalized greetings card or a place setting for a party table. Here, we have made a four-letter name card, but for more letters, simply increase the length of the card and fold it more times. You can colour the cats to look like a pet you know.

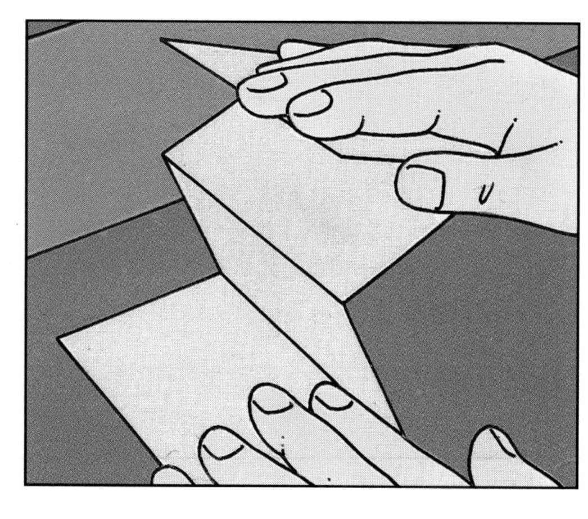

1 To make a name with four letters, cut a strip of card 32cm x 11.5cm (12¾in x 4½in). Fold the strip in half, then into quarters.

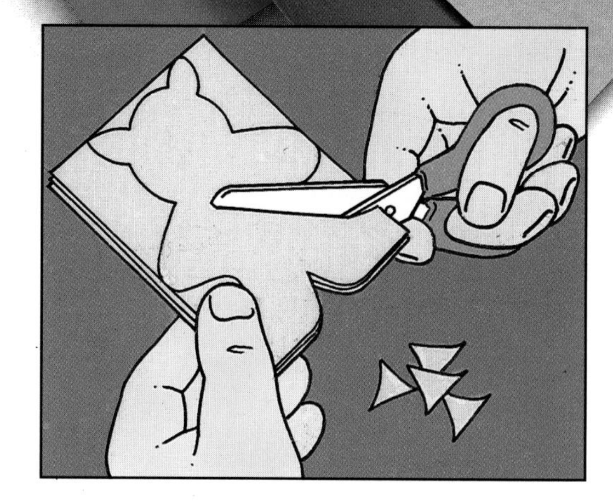

2 Using a pencil, trace the cat pattern on page 94. Turn the tracing over and hold it in position on the card. Rub firmly over the outline with a pencil. The cat pattern will appear on the card. Cut out the cat through all four layers, taking care not to cut along the folds.

3 Cut out the letters for the name from coloured gummed paper. You could trace around letters from a newspaper. Stick the letters on to the cats.

4 Draw the cats' faces with a black felt-tip pen then draw squiggles with a brown or orange felt-tip pen for the fur.

PARTY HATS

These party hats are ideal to make for a sunny, summer birthday party, or even for a New Year party when everyone is looking forward to their summer holidays. You could ask your friends to make one too, and give a prize for the best hat.

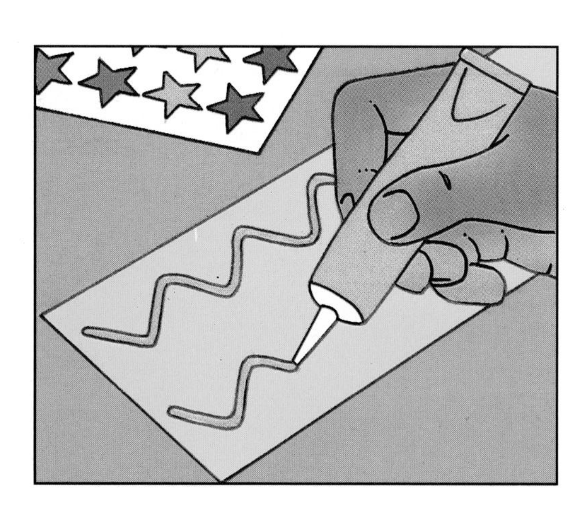

1 Cut out a strip of card 7.5cm (3in) wide and long enough to fit around your head. Decorate the strip with glitter pens and stickers.

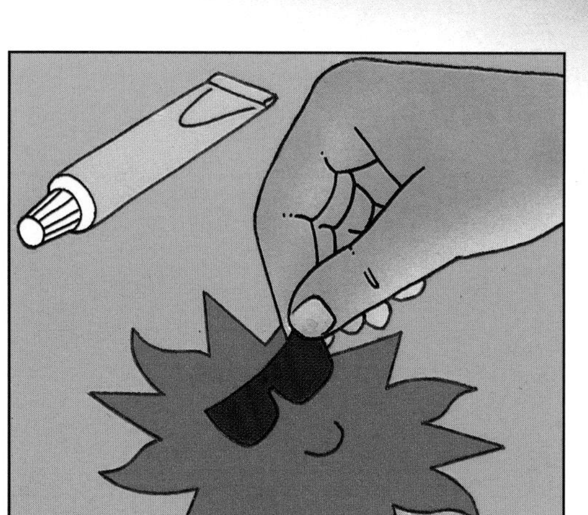

2 Using a pencil, trace the sun pattern on page 94. Turn the tracing over and position it on the card. Rub firmly over the outline with a pencil. The sun pattern will appear on the card; cut this out. Draw a smiling face with a felt-tip pen or glue on sunglasses cut from black card.

3 Decorate the sunrays with glitter pens then glue on some feathers in an upright position to the back of the sun.

YOU WILL NEED
Coloured and black card
Glitter pens and black felt-tip pen
Star stickers
Marabou feathers
All-purpose glue
Foam adhesive strip
Tracing paper and pencil
Scissors

4 Stick the sun to the middle of the card strip with a foam adhesive strip. Overlap the ends of the hat and glue together.

TREASURE CHESTS

These glittering jewellery boxes are encrusted with coloured gems, mounted on shiny sweet wrappers. Decorate these fabulous treasure chests in any pattern you choose. Make one to store your own jewellery, or as a present for a special friend.

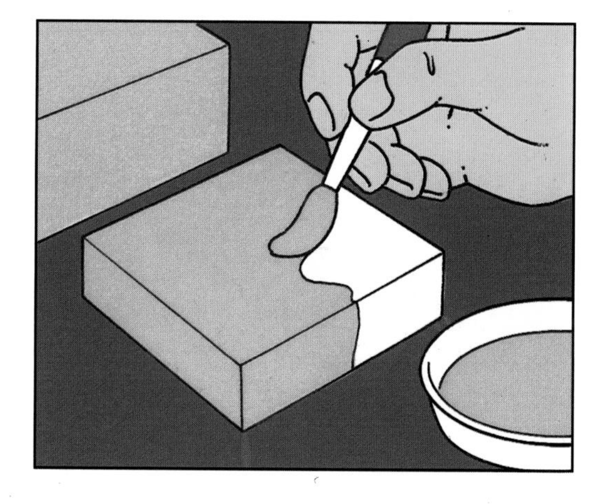

1 Paint the box and its lid with gold paint – it may need a couple of coats to get a good, rich gold colour. Leave the box to dry.

YOU WILL NEED
Cardboard boxes
Gold acrylic paint
Water-based varnish
Foil sweet wrappers and scissors
All-purpose glue and paintbrush
Coloured plastic or glass gemstones

2 Gently smooth out the sweet wrappers with your fingers. Cut them into squares and narrow strips. Take care, as these foil papers can tear easily.

3 Plan your design, placing some of the gems on the squares of foil. When you are happy with the design, glue the stones and foil in place on the lid of the box.

4 Coat the back of the foil strips with glue and wrap them around some of the large stones. When the glue has dried, varnish the box lid, including the gems. This will protect the surface.

HOLLY STOCKING

Here is a cheery stocking just right to hold a special little gift. By sewing a ribbon loop at the top, the stocking can be hung on the Christmas tree.

YOU WILL NEED
- Brightly coloured felt
- Green felt
- Pins and scissors
- Red ball-shaped button
- Red ribbon
- Tracing paper and pencil
- Fabric glue

1 Trace the stocking pattern on page 95 and cut out. Lay the pattern on to two layers of bright felt and keep it in place with pins or sticky tape. Carefully cut around the pattern – you will have two stocking shapes.

2 Cut a slit in one stocking at the top centre for a buttonhole. Pin the stockings together and sew around the edges, leaving the top open.

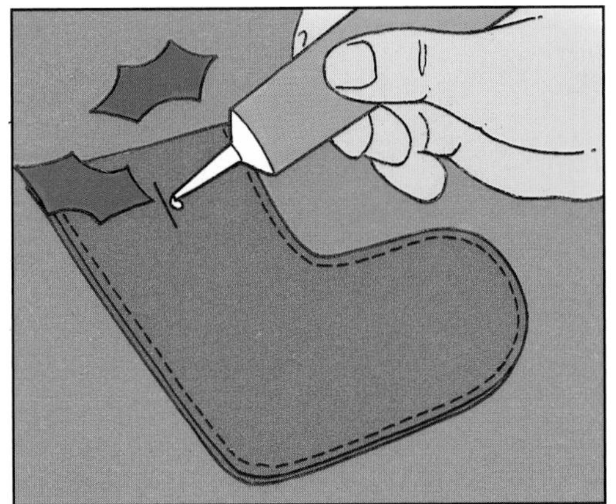

3 Cut out two holly leaves from green felt and glue one to each side of the buttonhole.

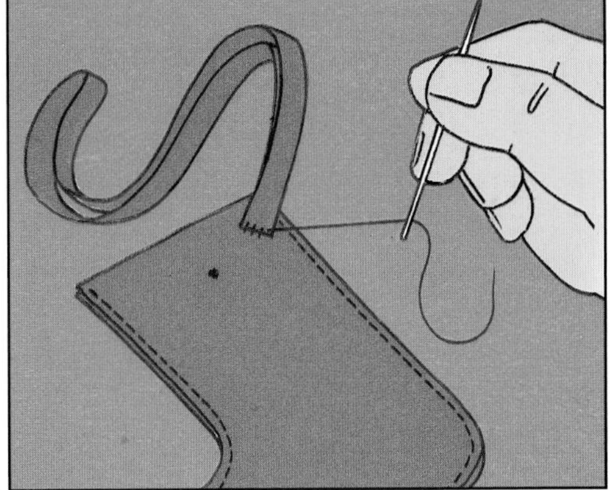

4 Sew the button to the stocking without the buttonhole, so that you can button the stocking up. Make a ribbon loop and sew the ends behind the stocking at the top.

SALT-DOUGH WREATH

Salt dough is like a bread dough and it can be made from basic ingredients in the kitchen cupboard. Use salt dough to make all sorts of decorations and ornaments like this Christmas wreath – but remember that you cannot eat it!

1 Put the flour and salt in the bowl and stir in the water a little at a time. Mix the ingredients with a wooden spoon to make the dough. Ask an adult to set the oven to Gas mark 3/325°F/160°C.

SAFETY TIP: *Make sure an adult helps you when using the oven.*

2 Sprinkle flour on the work top. Break off two pieces of dough and pull them into long sausage shapes. Twist the shapes together, as shown, then curve the dough into a circle and squash the ends together.

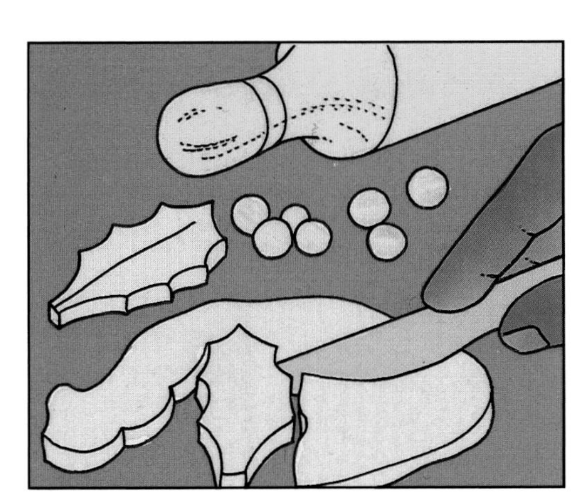

3 Roll some of the dough out flat and cut out holly shaped leaves. Roll extra dough into very small balls for berries. Put all the shapes on to a baking tray and bake them in the oven for about 30 minutes, or until they are hard.

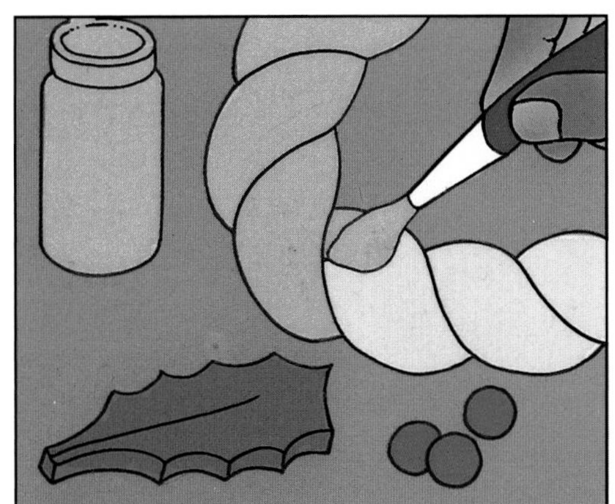

4 Wearing oven gloves, ask an adult to help you take the dough from the oven. Leave the dough to cool, then paint the leaves green, the berries red and the wreath a rich gold colour. Leave the paint to dry completely. Then add dashes of gold paint.

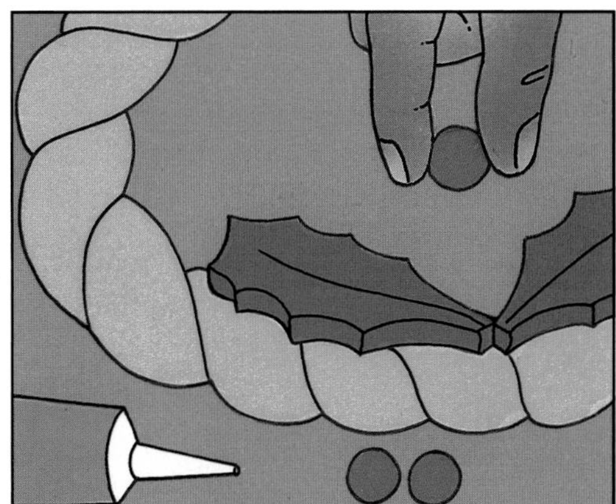

5 Glue the berries and leaves over the join in the wreath. Varnish the wreath and leave it to dry. Decorate the completed wreath with ribbons, securing them in place with dabs of glue. Make a loop of ribbon and glue it to the back of the wreath.

CHRISTMAS FRIEZE

Have you ever made paper dolls? This frieze is made in the same way, by folding the paper into rectangles, then cutting the shapes out all at once. The trick is to make sure that the shape you cut touches the folds at two or three points.

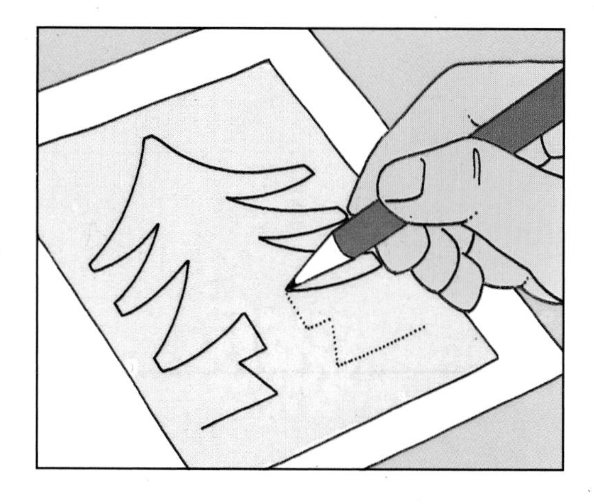

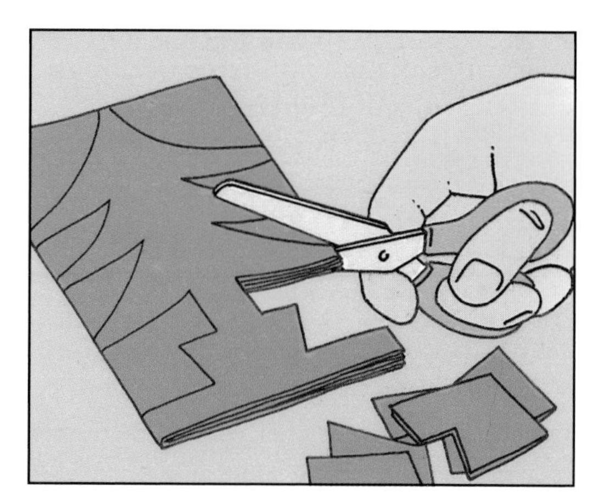

1 Using a pencil, trace either the bell or the Christmas tree patterns on pages 94 and 95. Turn the tracing paper over and lay it on a piece of scrap card. Rub firmly over the outline with a pencil. The pattern will appear on the card. Cut out the shape.

2 Cut a long strip of coloured paper 84cm (26in) long. Fold the strip in half from left to right three times.

3 Lay your pattern on the folded paper and carefully draw around it. Cut out the shape through the layers, but do not cut through the folds.

4 Pull open the frieze and decorate with glitter pens and shapes cut from gold paper. Glue the tinsel trims in place.

YOU WILL NEED
Coloured cartridge paper
Gold paper
Scrap card
Glitter glue sticks
All-purpose glue
Glitter and tinsel trims
Scissors and ruler
Tracing paper and pencil

PATTERNS

The following pages show the patterns you will need to make many of the projects in the book. To find out how to copy a pattern follow the step-by-step instructions given for each project.

You may want to make a pattern that you can keep to use again. To do this trace over the outline of the pattern with a pencil. Turn your tracing over and lay it on to a piece of thick card. Rub firmly over the outline with a pencil. The image will appear on the card. Cut out the shape. If you keep this pattern in a safe place, you can use it time and time again.

LIZZIE THE LIZARD

Page **14**

Body

Legs

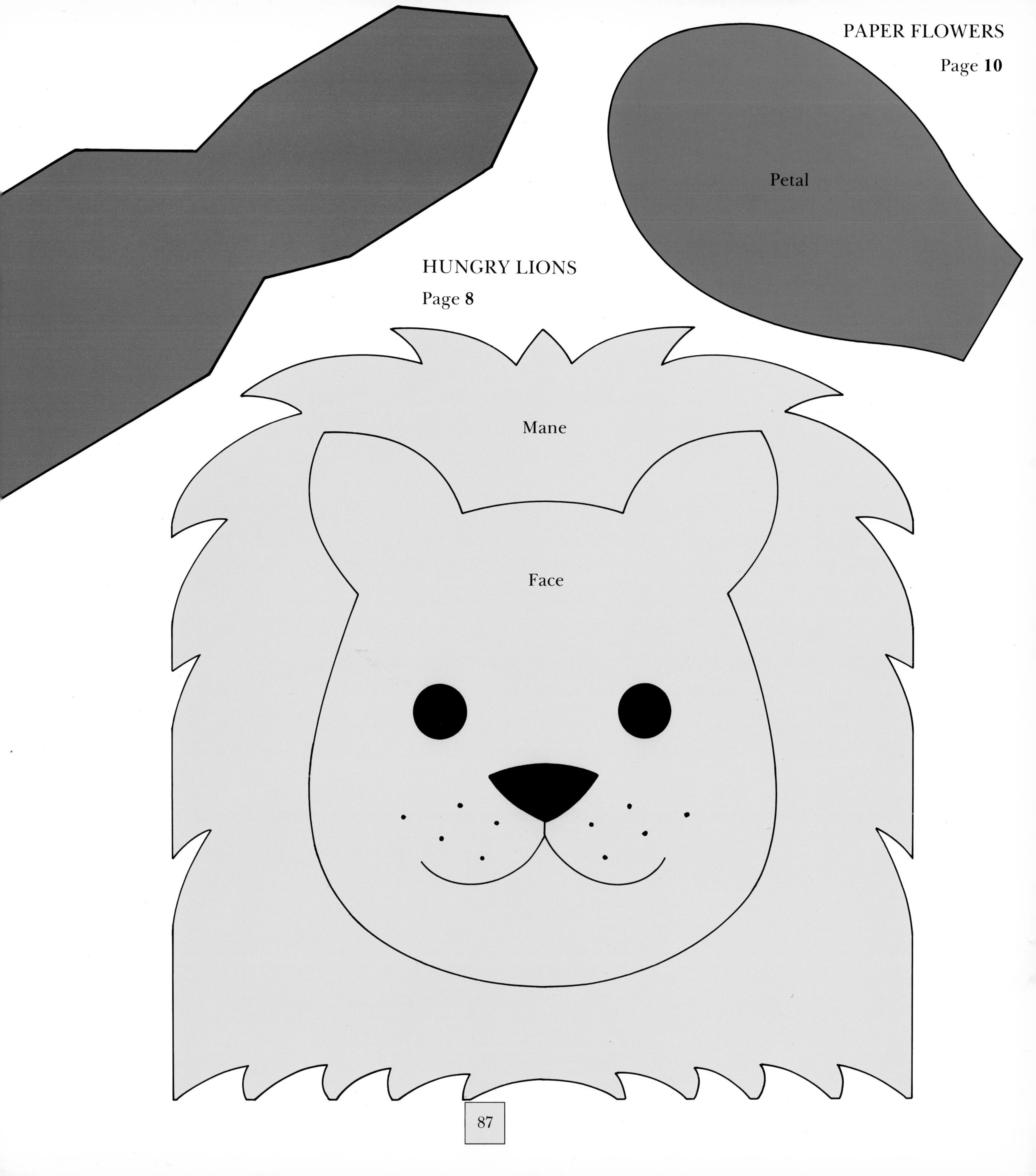
PAPER FLOWERS
Page 10
Petal
HUNGRY LIONS
Page 8
Mane
Face

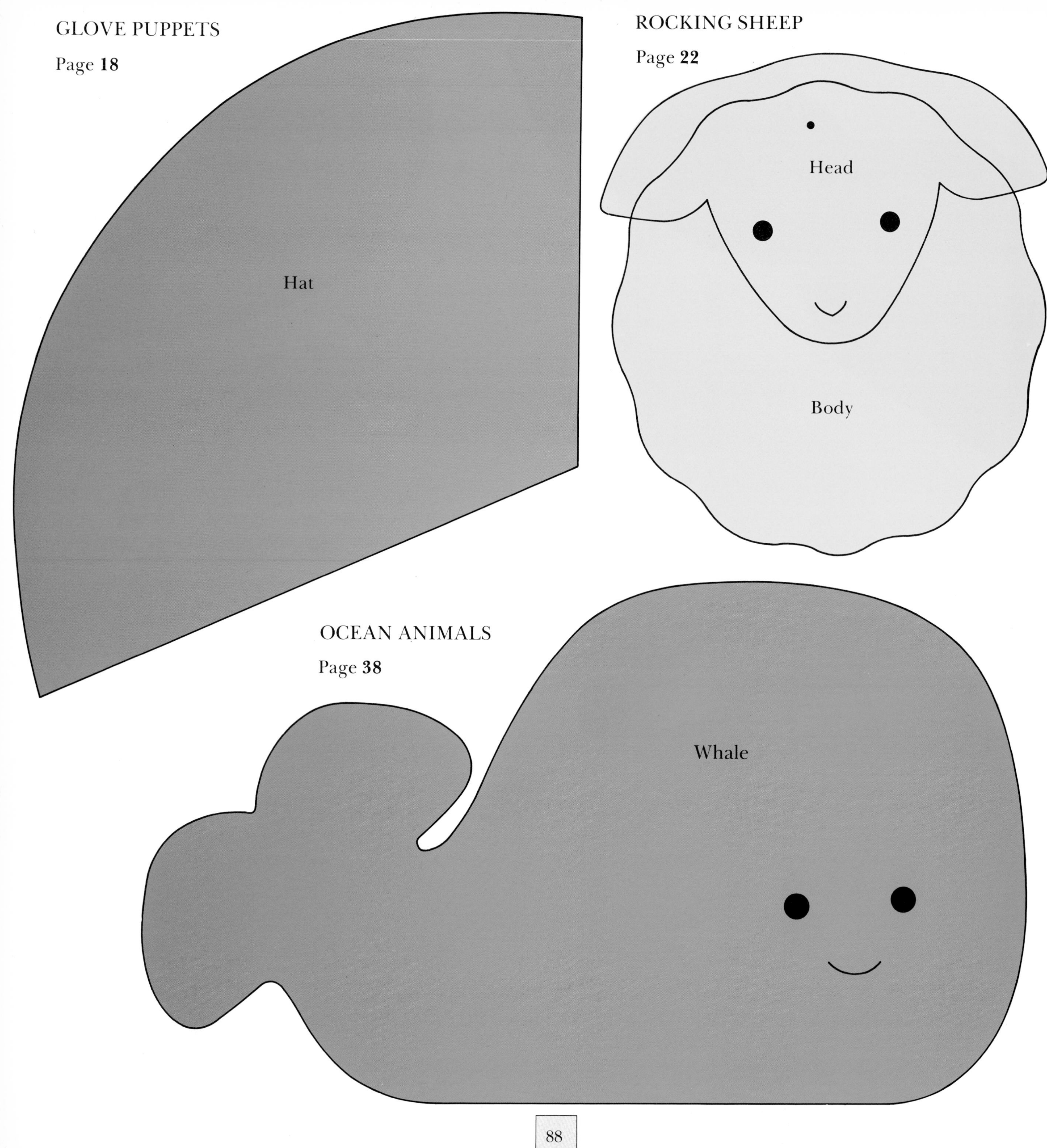
GLOVE PUPPETS
Page 18
Hat
ROCKING SHEEP
Page 22
Head
Body
OCEAN ANIMALS
Page 38
Whale

Page **36**

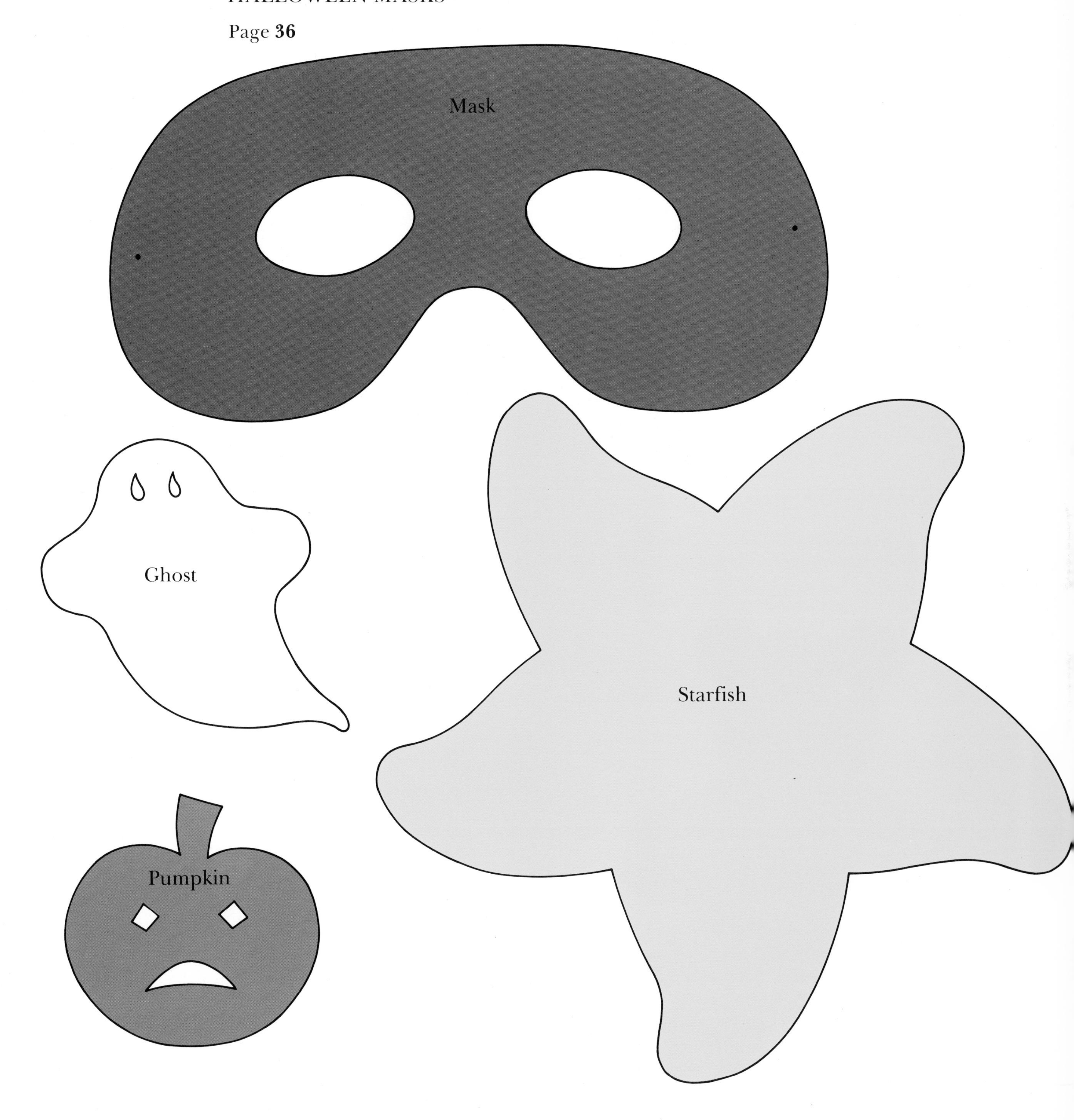

DINOSAUR BADGES

Page **40**

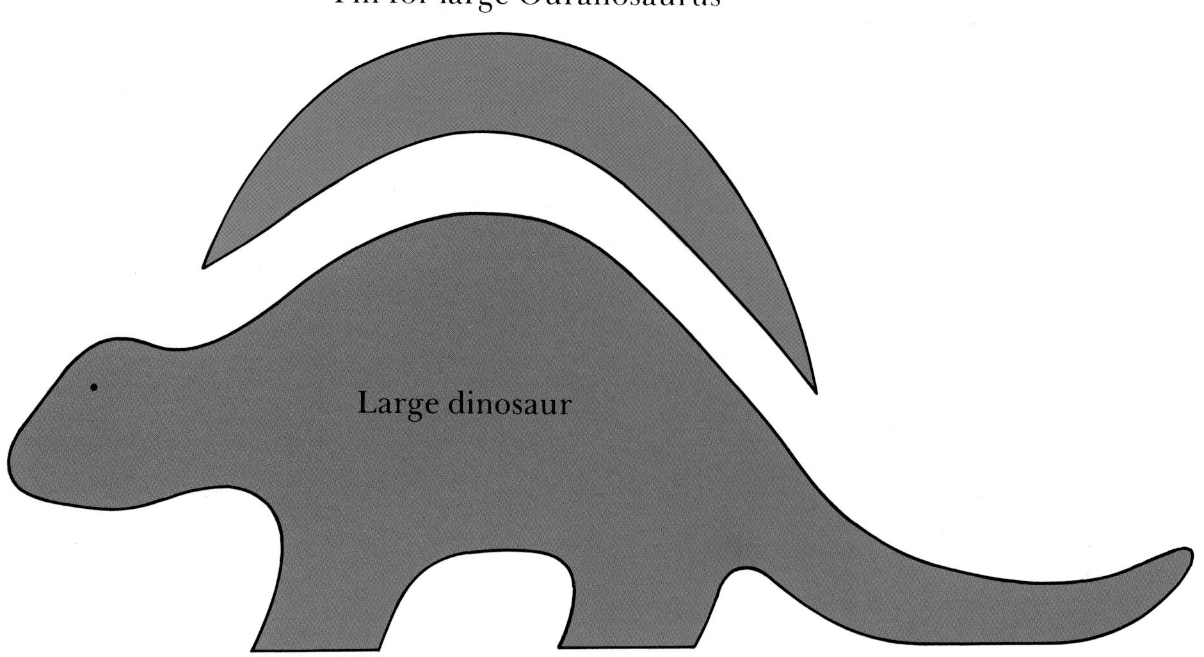

TEDDY TRIO

Page **48**

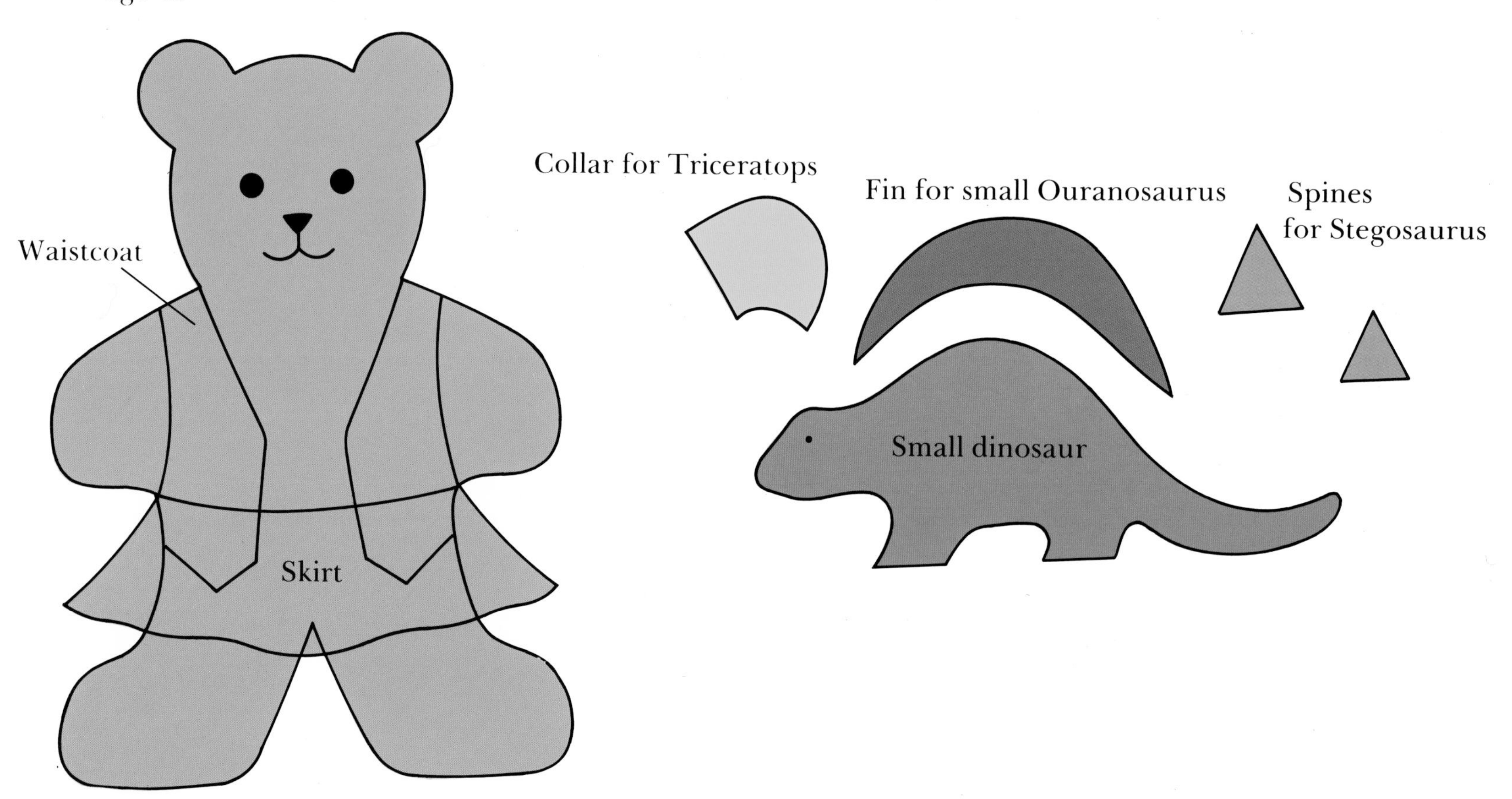

CLOWN COLLAGE

Page **50**

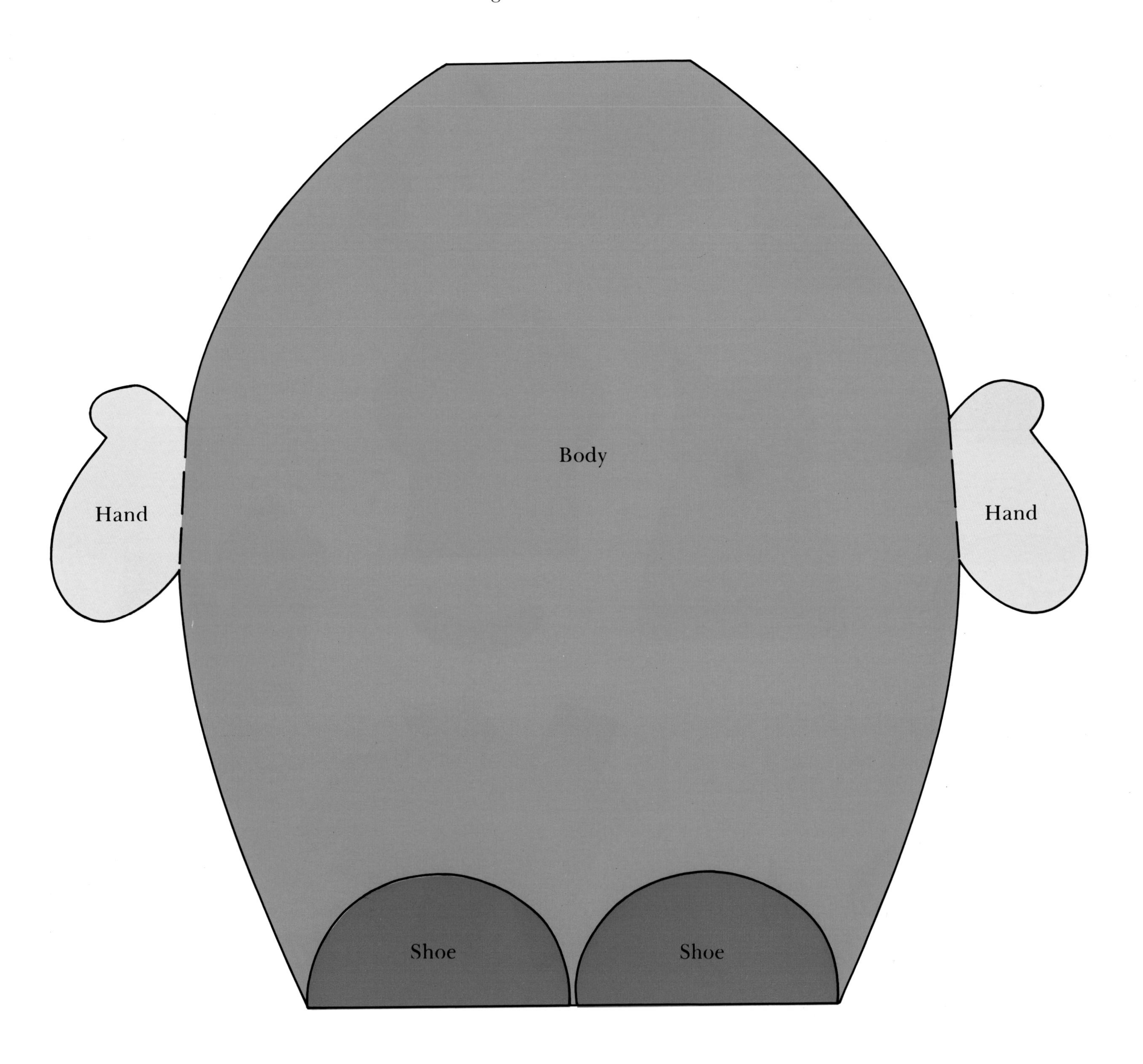

FINGER PUPPETS

Page **52**

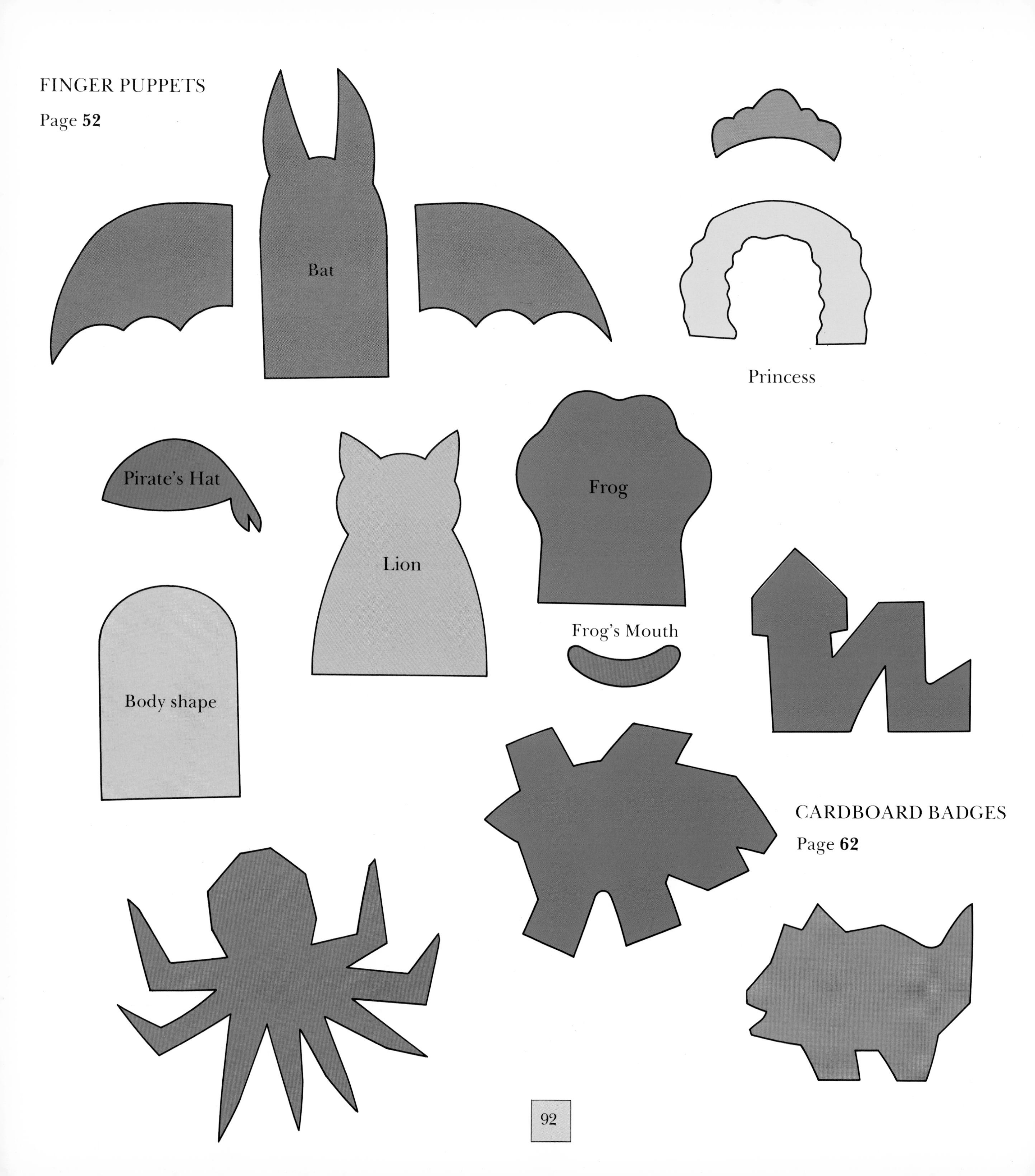

CARDBOARD BADGES

Page **62**

GLIDERS

Page **60**

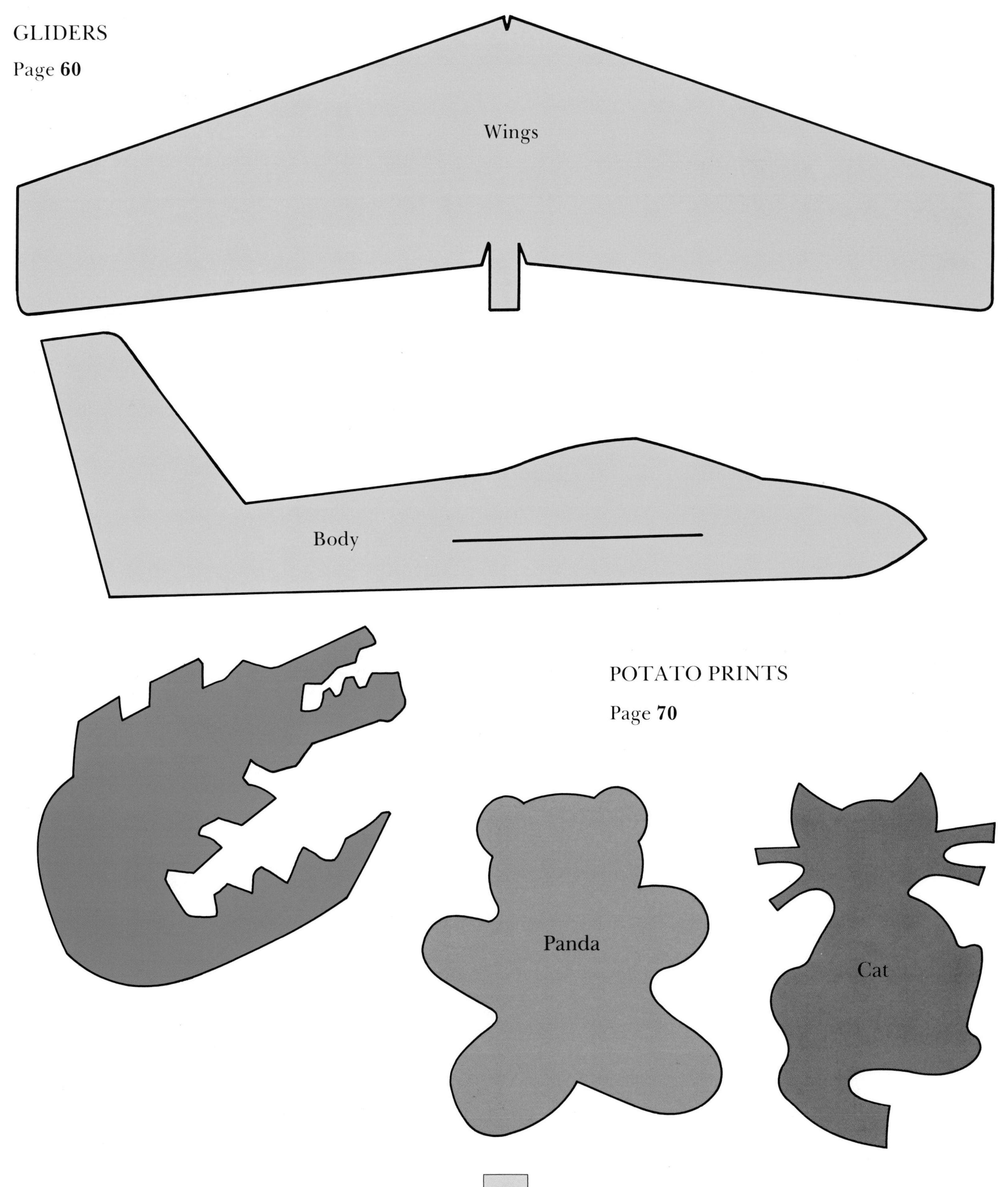

POTATO PRINTS

Page **70**

CONCERTINA CATS

Page **74**

Bell

Sun

PARTY HATS

Page **76**

CHRISTMAS FRIEZE

Page **84**

Tree

HOLLY STOCKING

Page **80**

INDEX

ACKNOWLEDGEMENT
The publishers would like to thank The Handicraft Shop, Northgate, Canterbury, Kent CT1 1BE, for their help in compiling this book.